John Sentamu's *Agape* Love Stories

John Sentamu's
Agape Love Stories

22 Stories of God's Love
Changing Lives Today

**Presented by the Archbishop of York,
Dr John Sentamu**

Stories written by
Carmel Thomason

DARTON · LONGMAN + TODD

First published in 2016 by
Darton, Longman and Todd Ltd
1 Spencer Court
140 – 142 Wandsworth High Street
London SW18 4JJ

Interviews conducted by Carmel Thomason

ISBN: 978-0-232-53223-4

A catalogue record for this book is available from the British Library.

Phototypeset by Kerrypress Ltd, St Albans, Hertfordshire
Printed and bound in Great Britain by Bell & Bain, Glasgow

Contents

1 Relationships that transform

Jean Vanier

Jean Vanier is the founder of L'Arche, an international network of 147 residential communities across 35 countries, where people with and without intellectual disabilities live and work together. In the UK alone, there are 11 L'Arche communities and a L'Arche project. Jean also founded Faith and Light, a network of 1,500 support groups in 82 countries that brings people with and without disabilities together, both through community and family gatherings. In 2015 Jean Vanier was awarded the Templeton Prize for his revolutionary contribution in affirming the spiritual dimensions of life through his practical works and insights; living his philosophy that people society typically considers to be the weakest can enable the strong to recognise and welcome their own vulnerability and humanity.

'Blessed be the God and Father of our Lord Jesus Christ, the Father of mercies and the God of all consolation, who consoles us in all our affliction, so that we may be able to console those who are in any affliction with the consolation with which we ourselves are consoled by God' (2 Corinthians 1:3-4).

John Sentamu writes:

Have you ever got lost when travelling abroad? As you struggle to make yourself understood, do you begin to be afraid that you'll never get home safely? What a blessing when someone appears who can understand you and who knows the way to guide you safely back to your route. The Father sent the Holy Spirit in the name of our Crucified, Risen and Ascended Saviour to be our Comforter who stands beside us and guides us, holding us up ready to face the world – a very present help in time of trouble. He is the One who responds to the call.

Jean Vanier's story shows how the Holy Spirit works through ordinary people like him – and us – to be that comfort and support to those who are lost. When Jean Vanier first saw those desperate men in the asylum, he was dismayed by how rejected and misunderstood they were. God reached Jean Vanier's heart through the men's cries for fellowship and friendship, and set him on a path that would transform their lives as well as his.

As Jean Vanier says, 'When we draw on God's love we can break down the barriers of fear, and be ready to meet with difference. We can find our way safely to a home in God's family where all are accepted and understood.' Knowing that we *'now see in a mirror, dimly, but then we will see face to face. Now we know only in part; then we will know fully, even as we have been fully known.'* (1 Corinthians 13:12).

✟

There's a passage in John's Gospel where Jesus heals a man who has been blind from birth. On first seeing the man, the disciples ask Jesus, 'Who sinned, this man or his parents, that he was born blind?' Jesus replies, 'Neither this man nor his parents sinned. This happened so that the works of God might be displayed in him.'

Sadly, the disciples' question echoes what for years many people believed – disability was a punishment from God and brought shame on the parents. Disability was something that mustn't be talked about for fear that if other parents knew they wouldn't want their children to marry into your family. I've seen the reality of these beliefs as recently as a few years ago, when our L'Arche community in Canada was asked by a local psychiatric hospital if a 70-year-old man called Louis could join them. From Louis' file we learned that he had brothers and sisters still living, so we rang to let them know about his new circumstances. Before taking our call, none of them knew that they had a brother called Louis and that he had been placed into the care of an institution.

I was into my mid-thirties before I met anyone with intellectual disabilities. I'd spent my early adult life as a naval officer but over time began to feel that it wasn't where I was meant to be. I left the navy not knowing what I was going to do, other than I had a strong call in my heart to follow Jesus. From there I met a priest, Père Thomas, who was chaplain of a small institution in the village of Trosly, in the Picardy region of Northern France where I now live. When I visited him at his work I was shocked to find that people were living closed off from the rest of society in this way. I started telling other people about this, wondering if there was something we could do to help. A parent of a disabled child told me that I should go and visit St Jean les Deux Jumeaux, an asylum for people with intellectual disabilities in the south of Paris.

I'm aware that today even the word 'asylum' has a brutal sound to it. St Jean les Deux Jumeaux was not a psychiatric hospital, it was an asylum that had grown out of an intention to ease the pain of parents without, as far as I could see, any thought for the wellbeing of those in its care. Any parent who rang up and said, 'I have a mentally disabled son and I don't know what to do,' would be told that there was a place for their child at St Jean les Deux Jumeaux. When I visited there were 80 men living there, crowded into two dormitories of 40. The men had no privacy and no work to occupy their time. The atmosphere was chaotic and there was a lot of violence. Discovering this world of pain and rejection left me reeling. I didn't know what to do. Although horrified by what I saw, I was touched by the people living there. As I left I heard, 'Will you come back? Will you be my friend? Will you write to me?' It was a cry for relationship that I couldn't ignore.

Thoughts of how those men were living stayed with me. To me, they were among the most oppressed of peoples. If being a disciple of Jesus was to be close to the poor, then I felt that these men were the people he was calling me to be close to. With the support of a few friends we were able to buy a little house near Compiègne and I explained to Madame Martin, the director of the asylum, that I would like to offer a home to two of its residents. She was supportive of the idea and we agreed that two men, Philippe and Raphael would come to stay with me in my home, initially for one month and then after that should they want to stay then they could.

For Philippe and Raphael to be liberated from this institution was super. Yet, as much as they were blessed by their change in circumstances, so too was I blessed by their friendship. I'd started off thinking that what I was doing was about helping people with mental disabilities but I began to realise that while they were being blessed because they now had good food and a comfortable place to live, I too was blessed by their friendship. I realised how easy it is for us to get caught up in a culture of individual success, of winning, of power, of knowledge and so on; often without realising we are doing it. None of that mattered for Philippe and Raphael. Simply being around them changed my view of the world and opened my heart.

It was 1964 and it felt like anything was possible. People were interested in and wanted community. The Vatican Council was opening out, the economy was growing and there was a general atmosphere that encouraged people to look at the world in a different way. Of course, there were people who thought that what I was doing was a bit crazy. What did it mean for a 36-year-old man to be living with two men from an asylum? What were my plans for the future? I didn't have any, except 'we shall see'. Other people in the village were touched by what they saw and I met a wonderful psychiatrist who helped me to understand more about mental disabilities.

About eight months after Philippe and Raphael came to live with me, I was asked to take over a small mental institution in the village. On arrival I found that the staff had all left and I was alone with 30 mentally disabled men who'd had years of being humiliated and were angry. Living with the reality of that is difficult. I also needed to learn about finance, salaries, legislation, working with government, all of the things that go with running an organisation and creating structure. A couple of people from the village came to help but it took some time for life in the institution to quieten down because the needs of the men at that time were so immense. There were painful moments but through the difficulties I began to understand that there is something about living with those who have been rejected and discovering their beauty that leads us to the whole of the message of Jesus, which is simply to love one another.

We called our community L'Arche (the Ark) and it grew in a spirit of craziness and fun. I say craziness because some were difficult people, and when you face difficulty you have to grow. As a community we were growing in love, we were together and there was a sense that all of this was worthwhile, that it's what the Gospel is about. The real work of Jesus is often something you don't see and don't realise is happening. For me, it wasn't a big road to Damascus change, but rather a gradual sense that I was beginning to accept people more than I did before. People I'd once found a pain in the neck I began to see as being on the same mission – to discover that, whatever our differences, we are all loved by God.

To see the transformation of people coming from institutions, through relationship, is beautiful. People came to us, they stayed and L'Arche grew from there. I had a sense that this work was being guided by God. An Anglican couple from Canada, Steve and Ann, were among the first people to live in the house. They were deeply touched and when they returned home they wanted to start a similar community. Things just happened. I went to India because I was invited and very quickly a community started there. It wasn't that we placed an advertisement to say come for X hours with a salary, it was something else. Everything was based on relationships that transform and it was this gradual transformation that brought me to the realisation that this is God's work. What is happening at L'Arche is not my work or the work of others. It is Jesus, showing us, somewhere in the whole of the mystery of the body of Christ, that those whom we may view as weak have been chosen by God: they put to shame the strong and the powerful (cf 1 Cor 1.27).

Even today assistants will come to L'Arche wanting to know what good they can do only to discover that this is not the question. It's a change of perspective, from a sense of superiority, to discover that what is important is togetherness, listening, understanding, and creating a culture of love and celebration where people feel wanted and accepted for who they are. Relationship isn't simply doing things for someone else, it's about revealing I'm happy to live with you and it's good to be together. When we are accepted for who we are, the revelation is more beautiful than we can dare believe. When people discover that they are valuable, it feels good to live.

By living with people who are fragile, we begin to learn what fragility is about. Intellectually it can be great, but in reality it's not always so easy to live with other people and I don't just mean with people with intellectual disabilities; relationships with other assistants can create tensions and jealousies. While living in community, assistants often discover their own fragility, weakness and difficulties, because at the heart of community is relationship and to have relationship you have to work at it.

Everything about L'Arche is about relationship – how to grow and accept people as they are, not wanting to change them but to rejoice in our differences. Today we have a lot of visits from young people who come to L'Arche for a day or a few days. Afterwards we ask each of them to write an evaluation. Most of them write that before coming to L'Arche they were frightened. In that fear is often something positive about wanting to do the 'right thing' so to speak. For example, the young people were frightened about how to meet people with disabilities; how to understand people if they don't talk; how to relate and feeling that they themselves don't really know how to relate. There are others who were fearful that the people living at L'Arche are crazy people and so on.

In a way their initial thoughts reflect our societies, which are often based on fear of difference. I have great concern in France now about the breakages between the original French population and the Muslim population. Our world can be one of divisions, breakdown and hatred, yet the tears of a Muslim woman are the same as the tears of a Christian woman. We might have different cultures and religions but we are all still very human and to be human is to be fragile; we are born to live but also born to die.

To meet with difference is to discover the world of barriers and fears. At L'Arche there is a breaking down of the fear of difference, the fear of weakness, and the fear of death because we have lived a relationship that transformed us. I see it as a breaking down of walls to become a place of peace and a sign of peace in the world. A place where people are allowed to be themselves; to realise that they are precious and to discover that every human being is precious, because somewhere in the heart of L'Arche is the desire of Jesus that we may be one.

2 A role to be played

Richard Taylor

Richard Taylor's ten-year-old son Damilola was killed in 2001 on the way home from an after-school club. Following Damilola's death, Richard and his late wife Gloria founded the Damilola Taylor Trust to bring positive change to inner city communities and increase the options and opportunities available to youngsters in those areas. In 2011, Richard was awarded an OBE for his services to the prevention of youth violence in the New Year Honours list. He dedicated the honour to Gloria and Damilola.

'Do not repay anyone evil for evil, but take thought for what is noble in the sight of all. No, 'if your enemies are hungry, feed them; if they are thirsty, give them something to drink' (Romans 12: 17, 20a)

John Sentamu writes:

The Apostle Paul's famous Chapter 13 of his First Letter to the Corinthians about love says, *'Love bears all things, believes all things, hopes all things, endures all things'* (1 Corinthians 13:7). In fact it describes the very characteristics we see in Jesus of Nazareth in the four Gospels.

Richard Taylor's story is full of the pain of loss, but also full of the love of God who has helped him bear and endure the murder of his young ten-year-old son, and then the death of his wife, and has brought hope for others as a result.

How can we bear this kind of pain and still love? Only through the grace of Jesus Christ and the power of the Holy Spirit. Richard found this, when he tried to find some way forward after Damilola was so brutally killed by boys not much older than himself.

Richard saw that young people in the community needed help to have hope for their future. He was able to turn his hurt and distress to practical ways of building up those young people so that they could become the people God meant them to be.

Jesus tells his followers that love is not just easy affection for those we like, but the difficult path of caring for those who hurt us: *'love your enemies, do good to those who hate you, bless those who curse you, pray for those who abuse you... Do to others as you would have them do to you'* (Luke 6:27-28, 31). Richard discovered the power of this kind of love and in doing so is changing lives.

✝

Damilola was our youngest child by ten years. We hadn't expected at that time in our lives to have another child, so when we learned Gloria was pregnant again we felt this child was a wonderful, precious gift from the Almighty. From the moment Damilola came into the world on 7 December 1989 we saw signs of that special gift. He was a brilliant boy who had friends of all ages. He had a smile that no-one could ignore because from it shone his love for life, with an infectious quality that made people want to be around him.

For the first ten years of Damilola's life we lived, as a family, in Lagos, Nigeria, where I worked as a civil servant. Our daughter Gbemi has a severe form of epilepsy, which today still affects her and us as a family. We heard that there were more successful treatments available in the UK, so in the summer of 2000, Gloria and our three children, Gbemi, aged 23, Tunde, aged 21, and Damilola, aged 10, flew to Britain so that Gbemi could go to King's College Hospital in London, for what was the best treatment in the world at that time.

I would have preferred for Damilola to stay in Nigeria and continue his education, but he insisted on joining his brother and sister in the UK, so that was it, the family went and I stayed behind in Lagos because of my work. In many ways our life in Nigeria had been privileged, in that our children had many opportunities, and naturally from that came big dreams for their futures. We had a comfortable home and Damilola had a private driver to take him to and from school. Now he was squatting at an auntie's house in Peckham and was confronted with lots of challenges he'd never experienced before, and the stories I was hearing were not good ones.

Around that time there were a lot of illegal immigrants hiding in the area and they were scared to be found out. Whenever kids saw new migrants arrive in the area they would ask them for money as protection fees. I told Damilola: 'Don't give any money to other kids so that you can go to school.' So, Damilola never carried any money to school, although the kids still asked him every day. Those kids were collecting money for older kids who were buying drugs from dealers – that was the kind of activity that was going on, but no one ever paid much attention to these kids, many of whom who were in care, separated from their parents and any family.

Listening to these stories, Gloria and I were concerned that Damilola was being bullied, but he never complained. He was a joyous child, focused on all the new experiences his environment was exposing him to, and the opportunities he hadn't had in Nigeria. He joined a computer club at Peckham library, where he would go after school, and he was excited about what he was learning. He told me on the phone: 'Daddy, I am going to do a lot of work. I am going to study medicine so that I can learn about epilepsy and help Gbemi.'

Three months after arriving in the UK, Damilola left the computer club at about 4.30pm as usual and never arrived home. CCTV footage shows him running in that direction, but only 500 yards from his front door he was attacked and stabbed in the thigh with a broken bottle. A workman, seeing a trail of blood, followed it to find Damilola slumped in a stairwell of a block of flats where he had collapsed, trying to make his way home. The glass had severed an artery and Damilola died from blood loss on the way to hospital. He was ten days away from his eleventh birthday.

I was at a meeting in the Parliamentary Secretary's office when I was told the news. It was Tuesday morning and a phone call came through for me. At first I refused to take the call because I had my own office and didn't expect to receive calls in the Parliamentary Secretary's office. The man with the phone insisted. 'This call is from the UK,' he said.

'What? What's happening?' I said, taking the handset. It was my son, Tunde on the other end of the line.

'Why are you calling me now? How did you get this number?' I asked him.

'I called your office and I think they transferred the call,' he said.

'What's going on?'

There was a pause on the other end and I knew something was very wrong.

'Damilola went to school yesterday and he didn't come home, he was stabbed to death.'

A scream came from deep inside me and then I must have passed out because I came round to see everyone standing around me. Luckily there was a doctor at the meeting and he was a kind man. Straight away he told the Parliamentary

Secretary that I should be allowed to leave and go to the UK. The same doctor arranged my travel and gave me $500 to use as expenses on the trip.

I am telling you right from the bottom of my heart that I cannot understand what happened. Damilola's killers were 13-year-old Ricky Preddie and his 12-year-old brother Danny. It deeply saddens me to think that a young person can take the life of another young person as if that life is nothing. After it happened people came to me talking about seeking revenge but I would send them away. I won't be pushed by other people to be involved in negativity and destruction in the community. I have to use my brain to be able to control the emotion, and the emotion is there still.

Many people were shocked and saddened by what happened, and shortly afterwards we were approached by Southwark Council who wanted to set up a charity in Damilola's name, whose work it would be to look into all the problems of young people in the area and try to do something about it. At the time our grief was still fresh so my response was: 'Just do what you want to do.' The charity was launched a year after Damilola's death. We were told that after a year the council would hand it over to the family and that is what happened.

During his three months in the UK Damilola kept a craft book of poems and drawings. I remember Gloria telling me on the phone: 'Your son is always on the carpet drawing.' When I looked at his papers I saw that he had been taking everything in about his new surroundings, but two things stood out to me. The first was a sketch of the hospital theatre where he one day hoped to work and the second was a short poem which read, 'I will travel far and wide to choose my destiny to remould the world. I know it is my destiny to defend the world which I hope to achieve in my lifetime'. When I read those words I felt a need deep inside me to fulfil the ambition of the young man. I'd lost my son because of the neglect and rot in the community; someone has to get up and do something.

Back in Nigeria I'd been involved in youth development programmes like setting up football clubs and sporting activities so I did have some experience to draw on. I also knew about the problems of the underprivileged children in Peckham, especially in the African Caribbean community. I couldn't understand how children had degenerated into this kind of lifestyle, but I knew that we needed to do something to help to support and improve the environment that these kids were living in. There was, and still is, a need to bring hope and happiness to the young people and to encourage them to make the most of their educational opportunities, because many of the youths in the area are excluded from schools for various reasons. There is a role to be played by everybody in that sense, the government, the council, the education system, the church, and maybe it's a role my family has been given too. As a result of Damilola's life, we now have a part to play.

Over the years the Trust has developed many projects to guide children and young people towards better choices in life, particularly those who may otherwise be vulnerable to gang and knife crime and those at risk of being kicked out of schools. For four years Gloria and I hosted the Spirit of London awards, funded by the Home Office and run by the Damilola Taylor Trust, to recognise the good work of some of the young people in the community we'd been supporting. We'd been helping open opportunities for young people to develop their potential, and some of them went on to build businesses of their own. We were also invited by King's College, London to be part of its access to medicine project for young people who have been unable to gain admission into mainstream medical school. Several of the young people who used the scheme have now graduated and are practising medicine in the UK and abroad, which is something that has made me happy.

Until she died in 2008, Gloria gave everything she had to the work of the charity. I believe that she died because of the pressure and heartbreak caused to her by Damilola's death – she loved him so much. Gloria bottled up her hurt. I am able to talk about my heartbreak, but she couldn't. After his death she was diagnosed with high blood pressure. One day as I was coming home I saw a crowd of people standing around a person on the ground. When I got closer, I could see it was Gloria; she'd had a heart attack and fallen to the ground. I travelled with her in the ambulance but I knew as soon as I saw her face that I'd lost her.

Gloria was 57 years old when she died. I've lost my son, my wife, and my job. My life will never be the same, but I am still alive. I believe that Gloria's spirit and Damilola's spirit are still alive and that they will be watching in fulfilment the achievements we've been able to do in Damilola's name.

I believe that through the Damilola Taylor Trust we are changing lives. We have done a lot to bring hope to the area and some young people are now benefitting from Damilola's tragic death. My joy is to believe that some other people are achieving what Damilola cannot.

3   *Destined to carry on*

Tuatagaloa Joe

Tuatagaloa Joe Annandale is Paramount Chief of Poutasi, a village on the south west coast of Upolu, Samoa, which was devastated by a tsunami in 2009.

'We know that God makes all things work together for good for those who love God, who are called according to his purpose' (Romans 8:28).

John Sentamu writes:

Sometimes we are called to live lives or to do jobs which we would much rather avoid. Jonah ran away from God's call to go on a mission to Nineveh. Only a storm and a great fish got him to where he should be.

Tuatagaloa Joe had not wanted to answer the call to be Paramount Chief of his clan, but he finally accepted the responsibilities of the role, and was wonderfully helped by his wife for many years before the disaster of a tsunami took the lives of both his wife and mother-in-law, as well as others in the village. As Paramount Chief he had to be strong for the whole community and his years of obedience to his call enabled him to continue to rebuild that community.

In Romans 8, the Apostle Paul writes about the persecution and suffering that the Christian community was undergoing. And yet he speaks of his certain hope that all will be brought close to the glory of Jesus Christ and that nothing can separate us from his love. All things that happen in the life of those he calls – even the hard things – will be used and blessed by God. I love the way The Living Bible has paraphrased Romans 8:33-39:

'Who dares accuse us whom God has chosen for his own? Will God? No! He is the one who has forgiven us and given us right standing with himself. Who then will condemn us? Will Christ? No! For he is the one who died for us and came back to life again for us and is sitting at the place of highest honour next to God, pleading for us there in heaven.

Who then can ever keep Christ's love from us? When we have trouble or calamity, when we are hunted down or destroyed, is it because he doesn't love us anymore? And if we are hungry or penniless or in danger or threatened with death, has God deserted us? No, for the Scriptures tell us that for his sake we must be ready to face death at every moment of the day—we are like sheep awaiting slaughter; but despite all this, overwhelming victory is ours through Christ who loved us enough to die for us. For I am convinced that nothing can ever separate us from his love. Death can't, and life can't. The angels won't, and all the powers of hell itself cannot keep God's love away. Our fears for today, our worries about tomorrow, or where we are – high above the sky, or in the deepest ocean – nothing will ever be able to separate us from the love of God demonstrated by our Lord Jesus Christ when he died for us.'

✠

In all the years we lived by the ocean, I never experienced anything like the tsunami which hit our shore on 29 September 2009. My wife Tui and I opened Sinalei Reef Resort and Spa on the south coast of Upolu in 1996. We designed it ourselves – a picture postcard vision of a tropical paradise, set on a white sand beach, shaded by coconut palms and looking out over the clear, turquoise waters of the Pacific Ocean. Here the weather is warm and tropical all year round. Very occasionally we get hit by a cyclone. We were once hit by a twister which spun past the house, picked up my fishing boat and dumped it just as quickly. That was the most unusual weather event I'd ever seen before the day of the tsunami.

Living by the sea you become familiar with its movements and rhythms. The tsunami happened just before seven o'clock on a Tuesday morning. We felt a rumble; what we didn't know at the time was that 170km off the coast to the south of us, an undersea earthquake with a magnitude of 8.3 had ruptured the fault line in the Tongan Trench. Within a few minutes the water receded with such speed that it looked like the sea was being emptied out and for a moment all we could see was coral and jumping fish. When the sea moves too fast for the fish to keep up you know you're in trouble – we knew then that a tsunami was coming and we needed to move fast.

We shared our home with Anna, Tui's 95-year-old mother, and her nurse, Tafa. As quickly as we could, we helped my mother-in-law into her wheelchair and out to the car. I was aware that every second counted and once we were all in I hit the accelerator to drive us to high ground. We'd only got 50 metres from the house when a wall of water 20 feet high appeared to our left. For a split second I thought that the house on that side of us might break the wave and shield us from its force, but just as we pulled in behind the house hoping for shelter the sea approached with a roar and speed that I never could have imagined. It buried the house first then us, picking up the car in its force. The tsunami came as three terrifying walls of water, the force of which sucked Tafa and then Tui from the car. We tossed around in the water, smashing against many trees and other objects before the wave carried us across the river another 300 metres inland.

When the car finally came to a standstill the water line was around my neck, and Tui's mother, who'd been sitting in the front passenger seat, was floating next to me. I saw two young boys on dry land and cried out for them to help me. Together we managed to get Anna out of the car through an opening in the window. I carried her to dry land and the boys kindly let me rest her in their wheelbarrow in which they carried her, running to their home on higher ground where their family nursed her. I had lost sight of Tui and Tafa after they were thrown from the car, so with my mother-in-law safe I set out to find them.

It was chaos. What had been the village, now looked like a lake – the usually lush vegetation was covered in water, with only the tree tops visible. I thought that Tui would be looking for me too and might have made her way back home, so I swam across the river and back towards our house on the coast. When I got there I found the house destroyed and there was no sign of Tui anywhere. By now the water had begun to subside, once again leaving fish jumping all over the place on the dry land. I walked back up to where the car had been swept. As I got close a group of young boys pointed in my direction and the atmosphere felt ominous. One of the boys came towards me and said: 'I think we know where Tui is.' I followed him to a tree, where he pointed upwards. I lifted my head and there was Tui trapped in the branches above.

I couldn't reach her so I had to go and ask someone for a machete to cut away the branches to free her. As I hacked at the tree I already knew it was too late. My beautiful wife had passed away – she'd drowned when the wave dragged us under. I managed to get Tui down from the tree and the boys helped me carry her 300 metres to higher ground. The hospital had been damaged too and people were taking the bodies of those who had perished to a shed next to a village shop, so that's where I carried Tui, to be identified among the dead. It was a terrible experience – there was wailing and a trauma that shook the whole village. In total 143 people died in the tsunami, 9 of whom, adults and children, were from our village.

My car was too battered and damaged to drive but there were other people on the higher ground with vehicles, so I hired a pick-up that took Tui and me to our hotel about 15 minutes away. When we arrived I saw that was a mess as well – the tsunami had done enormous damage. Thankfully our two children, who live on the other side of the island, hadn't been affected, but I knew I needed to contact them to tell them the devastating news. My son was on his way back from a trip to New Zealand but my daughter had already heard what happened and drove over to the Southside immediately.

Our tradition is to bury family members within 24 hours and that's what we did with Tui. At five o'clock the following morning we gathered for a service at the cocoa plantation where I grew up. It's now looked after by one of my nephews, but it is where Tui and I lived many years of our 40 years together. After my parents retired, we took over the lease and revived the plantation. We had a lovely homestead there and it was important to me that it was the setting for Tui's final service, after which we laid her to rest in our 'freehold' property further down the road where one of my sisters and a nephew are also buried. Tui's mother passed away in hospital a few days later.

Tui and I met at university and were married for 40 years. She was a wonderful and beautiful woman inside and out, being crowned the very first Miss Samoa beauty queen in her younger days. We were a partnership in every sense, bringing up our family and building a business together. Tui was also a huge support when I was appointed to be Paramount Chief. In many ways the role wasn't one that I took to easily. In Samoa we have a strong culture based on family. A group of families make up a clan, and each clan has a head – he is the Paramount Chief, and because of the village connection on my dad's side I became the Paramount Chief of my clan.

My heritage is what Samoans call 'afakasi', meaning I come from mixed ancestry. My father is half-Samoan, half-Scottish, and my mother is half-Samoan, half-Swedish. We grew up on our cocoa plantation with a lot of animals including horses, dogs, cats and milking cows, but with European values, and went to school like everybody else. In a way it was a very privileged upbringing, in that my parents had the freedom to send me off to school and I got to experience life in a way that is not always possible in a village setting with constraints of protocol and tradition. When my predecessor died, the family came together to choose a successor from five nominees. I wasn't one of them because I'd declined the offer feeling that I didn't know enough about village life. My cousin, who was a member of parliament in Samoa, was put forward instead.

The debate over which of the nominees should be Paramount Chief went on for nine years. Before a decision was made my cousin was assassinated. The tragic circumstances left my side of the family without a nominee and my uncle said: 'Joe, you're going to have to step up – we know you said no, but we're going to have to put your name up.' I agreed but my appointment wasn't straightforward. There was no family consensus as to which of the nominees should take the role and eventually I was appointed by decision of the court.

It took a long time to get the rest of my clan to accept me as the head of the family, and Tui played an enormous part in making that happen by winning the hearts of my family and also the women in the village. Here in Samoa, women are the heartbeat of the community, they raise the families and they do a lot of work in the church and community. Tui played a huge role in organising women in the village to support this work, and if we had guests in the village she was the one who organised the formal functions and the preparation of the food. In every way she made my role much easier for me. I didn't know how I could carry on leading the village without her by my side.

In times of trauma all sorts of things go through your mind and it did occur to me, I have to confess, that I should leave the village. I wasn't the only one in the village who had lost someone dear and as Paramount Chief it was important that

I appeared strong, but I wasn't sure that I could do that. I was walking around in a daze, as if I were hoping that this wasn't really happening.

After the funeral many of my friends and family offered to help me. One of my cousins in Hawaii asked me to spend Christmas with her and her family. I said: 'I'll come, but I won't spend Christmas.' Within a few days I was packed, and my family was happy that I was going away. I had a wonderful week there and when I came back I packed up again to visit my sister in Australia. My older sister, who has spent a lot of time in England and Scotland, joined us and we had a beautiful Christmas together. When I returned to Samoa my sister, Sose, who now runs the hotel, my sister-in-law, Jackie, and my kids had come a long way with re-building my house. Time away had given me time to reflect and when I saw what they'd done I wanted to carry on with the re-building so that I could move back home.

The whole of Poutasi had suffered extensive damage. The wave washed away everything in its path, including the district secondary school that was reduced to a concrete slab. Following the tsunami, most of the people whose homes were affected moved to higher ground. I thought about it too, but I had so many happy memories in my beach house that there was no way I was going to live anywhere else. I know that a lot of people thought that without Tui I would just pack it all in but I didn't. To do that would have been to turn my back on everything we had built up together and to turn my back on my role as Paramount Chief and the people who were looking to me for guidance through this devastating time. Once I'd had time to reflect it became very clear to me that being Paramount Chief was my calling – I couldn't just leave this place, I had to sit down and listen to what people were saying and what they were offering.

I was amazed by the outpouring of sympathy and support for our people. There were all sorts of people and organisations from all over the world wanting to help and I wasn't going to turn my back on that sympathy and help. I was destined to carry on with the village and with my responsibilities as head of the clan. I prayed a lot – that's where I get my strength – and spurred on by the strong call I felt to carry on, I did just that.

So much monetary aid was coming our way that I felt there ought to be formal, legal structures developed to manage it, so I formed the Poutasi Development Trust. Again I felt that Tui was helping me, because the monetary donations allowed us to continue the village projects that she had started before she passed away. Seeing those projects begin to flourish gave me the courage and the means to start others and soon there were more ambitious projects underway like a pre-school, a library and an arts and crafts centre.

A friend of mine from Wellington, New Zealand wanted to build something in Tui's memory. I wanted that too, but I also knew that Tui would have wanted me to think about the other people who had also lost someone dear that day, so we built a Memorial Hall in memory of Tui and the eight other members of our village who passed away that day.

Recently God has brought a new lady into my life called Tammy. We met at the Hash House Harriers running club, which I set up 35 years ago. There is an organised run every Monday and over the years the club has developed its own traditions that for me are a celebration of life and all its God-given wonders. Every week we see something new because we meet in a different location, and after a tough run we drink coconuts to quench our thirst, the host puts on a barbecue, we have a committee that takes care of the drinks, I play my ukulele and we sing.

4 Challenging perceptions

Jill Quinn

Jill Quinn is a founder and CEO of charity Dementia Forward. Established in 2012 its mission is to provide a fully-integrated local service, offering practical advice, support and information to promote the wellbeing of people whose lives are affected by dementia.

'Lord, you have searched me and known me. You know when I sit down and when I rise up; you discern my thoughts from far away. You search out my path and my lying down and are acquainted with all my ways' (Psalm 139:1-3).

John Sentamu writes:

If you're a keen user of Facebook, somewhere in cyberspace there will be thousands of pieces of information about your identity – where you've been on holiday, your scores on online games; your opinions on everything from the ice cream you just ate, to the Refugee Crisis. The dismay expressed by people who've lost their phone, and their Facebook entry has to be heard to be believed! But it's all retrievable if they can only go online again and call it all up – they know who they are again!

Sadly, as we see in Jill's story, life is not always so simple. Her story tells of the pain and loss of people losing their identity through dementia, and the family's suffering as they see their loved one disappearing. But her story also tells of the loving help that can make a difference.

Psalm 139 gives us comfort in knowing that our identity, our being, is in God's safekeeping. He who made us, knows even more about us than we do ourselves; he knows every detail of our past and our future. 'For we *have died and our life is hidden with Christ in God'* (Colossians 3:3), and we will never be lost to his love. *'When Christ who is our life is revealed, then we will be revealed with him in glory'* (Colossians 3:4).

☩

Imagine wearing your identity as a striped tie. Pieces of information about you are arranged randomly on the different stripes – your name, your birthday, your favourite place, what you enjoy doing – all things that go into making you who you are. Now, what if the tie was to rip in a random place and you couldn't remember the parts of your identity that had been written there? If you can't remember your birthday, does that mean it's no longer your birthday? What if you can still play honky-tonk on the piano but you can't remember the name of your closest friend? That is what it's like for someone with dementia. Their identity is still there, but they can't articulate it.

Take a simple pleasure like a cup of tea. What if you couldn't tell me how you like your tea? You like strong white tea with sugar and every day I bring you milky tea with no sugar because

I don't know any different. One day I bring you your tea and it's welcome because you're thirsty. You take a sip and it isn't what you expected. You want a drink but you can't drink that – it tastes awful. In frustration you throw the contents of the cup on the floor. I write on your care plan that you are aggressive, uncooperative and have a bad fluid intake. This information then affects how you are treated and the freedoms you're allowed – all because I didn't know how you like your tea. It's a caricature, I know, but when parts of someone's identity begin to fall away, it's our job as family, friends and neighbours to help hold the tie together for as long as we can.

At Dementia Forward, when we begin working with someone with dementia, we start by putting together a pen portrait of who they are. It's sketchy, but it's the kind of thing you might have written on your identity tie. For example, if a man is called Harold but prefers to be known by his middle name of Joe, then it's important people know to call him Joe. If we know his favourite place is Brimham Rocks, we can go there with him for a day trip. He may not remember that his birthday is 9 April, but when that day comes around we can wish him many happy returns and help him celebrate.

Unfortunately there is still a stigma about dementia that often even stops people sharing their diagnosis with friends and family. Unlike diagnoses of many other diseases, many people don't talk about it which means that they don't get the support they need at an early stage. They can't keep up with conversations at family gatherings, but instead of letting other people know why, they stop joining in and their lives shrink back. This happens with activities too. Someone may still physically be able to play golf but may never play again because they can't find their way around a golf course. Or, maybe a person has shopped and cooked for their family all their adult life but is no longer able to handle money so doesn't get to enjoy the experience of going to the butcher's shop and choosing a cut of meat.

It is understandable why family and friends want to protect loved ones who have been diagnosed with dementia, but often they become over-protective and it can be both frustrating and disabling for the person they are trying to help. It's common to hear a woman say: 'I can't remember the recipe but I can still stir something in a pan and he won't even let me near the stove.' Or I often hear a husband say of his wife: 'She won't even give me money for my pocket. I put my hand in my pocket and there's no change there. It doesn't feel right that I don't have any money.'

I'll then ask his wife: 'How much would it be worth to you, if you could make Fred happy?' Usually she'll say, 'I'll do anything'. I'll say: 'Would you be willing to let him lose £5 a week?' If his wife can afford it, of course she would. It sounds so straightforward, but when we are wrapped-up in caring for someone it can be easy to forget to ask them, 'What would you like?' and to really listen to that answer – to understand, as far as is possible, what care is like from their point of view.

Dementia isn't the same for any two people, so every time you meet someone who's had a diagnosis you have no idea where their journey is going to go and, if you're supporting them, where yours will go either. I wish that people would stop thinking of dementia as a natural part of ageing and see it for what it is: a disease. At Dementia Forward we work with lots of younger people with dementia, many of working age, some in their forties. One of our jobs has become supporting them to continue physical activities they enjoy, like swimming, walking and cycling. When we climbed Pen-y-ghent together I remember thinking, this is not what I thought dementia support was about; so we are often challenging perceptions, even our own. Our job is to listen to what people want and to enable them to do those things.

Sometimes it can be very difficult when you are close to a situation to see the small changes that could make life easier. As part of our support often we'll ask one of our support advisers or our Admiral Nurse (a mental health nurse who specialises in dementia) to spend a few hours with a family and observe patterns of behaviour that might inadvertently be triggering problems. For example, one couple who came to us for advice had always enjoyed eating breakfast sitting at a table, set beautifully with a crisp white linen cloth, fresh flowers and bone china crockery. As the wife's illness progressed she struggled to use a knife and fork and began to find the ritual she had once enjoyed a cause of frustration. Noticing this, the support worker said: 'Do you realise that every day you are starting off with an argument simply because you are trying to maintain this habit of eating your breakfast a particular way, when you could just sit in front of the TV, have a piece of toast and start the day off nicely?'

We've made it central to our work, to listen to what people want; to talk to them about their illness and how it affects them. Sometimes the tiniest things can make a huge difference to someone's life. At the moment we're all busy knitting 'Twiddlemuffs'. It's a funny name, but it is also a good description of what they are – thickly knitted woollen muffs with items such as ribbons, large buttons or textured fabrics attached on the inside and outside that people can twiddle. We've got volunteers all over knitting them for us using scraps of wool and old buttons. Twiddlemuffs cost the charity very little, but they can make a huge difference for someone with dementia who has restless hands and is finding it difficult to relax. Recently a man came into our office seeking help. His wife, who has dementia was agitated and couldn't settle. It was clear he was at crisis point and seemed surprised when one of our staff said: 'It's okay. You go and have a chat with a support adviser and your wife can stay with us. We'll have a cup of tea.' We gave his wife one of our twiddlemuffs. We weren't sure if she would like it, but she put her hands inside it and began exploring the different sensations of different textures and materials. When her husband came back into the room he was amazed at how much calmer she was. That's why it's important for us to have places locally where people can drop in, if they are in need of some support or advice. For our team, spending that time with the couple was a small thing to do, but for the man and his wife it made a huge difference to their day and they were incredibly grateful.

It is easy for relationships to start to fall away when someone has dementia. That is why being there for people is so important and why we organise weekly rather than monthly activities. If you've got dementia and you have a hospital appointment on the same day as a monthly activity then it could be two months before you saw your friends again. I hear people coming out of our singing group saying: 'This is the best day of the week. I love coming here.' Some of that is the uplifting experience of the music, but a lot of it is regularly meeting up with other people who understand and building friendships. It's the same for all of our groups. They are light-hearted. It's about enjoyment and being in a place where you don't need to explain because the other people there understand dementia. We have a knitting circle and sometimes women will come along even if they are no longer able to knit. If you've always knitted and enjoy it, you can still hold the knitting; you can still join the group, because while you are sitting in the circle when other people knit you are still part of the circle.

I wish that communities could be more dementia friendly so that people with dementia could join an established singing group, a walking group, whatever activity they are interested in. That would be the ideal. We're not there yet and sometimes it feels like we are just sweeping the surface of what's possible for people with dementia. Hopefully by being a visible support in the community we are changing perceptions, showing that the whole person is still there and we are holding that tie of identity together to give people with dementia the same respect and quality of life that everyone deserves.

5   The knock-on effect

Beverley Thomas

Beverley Thomas's twin daughters Charlene and Sophie Ellis were outside a party in the early hours of 2 January 2003 when four men pulled up in a car and opened fire with a MAC-10 machine gun and two automatic 9mm pistols, killing 18-year-old Charlene and her friend Letisha Shakespeare, 17. Sophie, her cousin Cheryl Shaw, and friend Leon Harris were all seriously injured in the gang-related attack. For more than a decade, Beverley has campaigned tirelessly to raise awareness of the problems of gang culture and to help rid Birmingham's streets of gun crime.

'Let love be genuine; hate what is evil, hold fast to what is good; Bless those who persecute you; bless and do not curse them' (Romans 12: 9, 14).

John Sentamu writes:

Sometimes when we read the Bible it seems as though throughout the whole of history, people have been going through grief, sorrow, and the bitterness of loss. When we hear stories like Beverley's we wonder if things will ever change and we ask where does our hope come from? Where is justice and peace?

The Bible answers us – *'our hope comes from the Lord'* (Romans 15:13).

The God of Justice is the same God who, while human beings were still his enemies, sent his Son Jesus Christ to die, rise and reconcile us to himself. We thank God that his justice comes with mercy, forgiveness and love to restore us.

Beverley's life was devastated when her daughter Charlene and Charlene's best friend Letitia Shakespeare were killed, and Beverley's daughter Sophie badly injured. But in time God helped her find a way towards restoration, which brought blessing not only for herself, but also for young people like the ones who had killed Charlene. It is a blessing that has also helped her daughter Sophie to understand the power of restorative justice

Lily Tomlin says, Forgiveness means giving up all hope for a better past'. It also means having hope for a future where love triumphs over hatred. For love is more powerful than hate. New life more powerful than death. *'The power and sting of death have been swallowed up in the victory of our Lord Jesus Christ'* (1 Corinthians 15:54-56).

✠

Before this happened to my family I knew nothing about gang violence. When you grow up somewhere like an estate all the kids grow up together, they tend to go to nursery and school together, so as a mother you see them all as friends. I never imagined some of those same kids would one day carry weapons that could spray bullets across the streets of

Birmingham killing people indiscriminately. So many innocent people get caught up in the feuds of rival gangs. Nobody thinks something like that could happen to them, until it does.

My twin girls Charlene and Sophie are the youngest of my four children and growing up were always quiet, homely girls. On New Year's night, 1 January 2003, they asked me if it would be okay to go to a nightclub. They'd never been to a nightclub before. I thought about it, they were 18 years old and, although still living with me, in the eyes of the law they were adult women. It wasn't as if they would be alone, there were four of them with their friend, Letisha and cousin Cheryl. I thought, okay, just this one time is fine, after all it's not New Year's Eve. All they were asking was to go to a nightclub with their friends, something thousands of young people do every night of the week. I agreed in a, 'yes, you can go, but don't ask me again', kind of way. Charlene didn't get to ask me again.

Where my daughters got shot is not where they left my house to go. I'd agreed they could go to a night club in Solihull, I knew nothing about a party somewhere else after that. I waited up for them coming home and as the evening crept into the following day I kept looking at the clock and wondering where they'd gone.

I had no idea when to expect them home. I was watching a film when the phone rang at five minutes to four in the morning. I tutted as I answered the phone, what time did they call this? There was a girl's voice at the other end. She said that she was a friend of Charlene and Sophie and she'd gone into one of their bags, found the phone and rang me. 'Your girls have been shot,' she said. My first thought was why would somebody want to go and shoot those two? I didn't know how serious it was, but my brain was trying to look for a reason. What did they do? They must have offended someone to go and get shot.

I put the phone down and called my mum who lives up the road. While at my mum's house I saw an ambulance drive by with blue lights flashing but no siren. When my mum and I got to City Hospital it was like the whole party had arrived before us and was spilling out of the corridors. After that, everything turned into a blur. I was there with all of these people and then someone took me to the back of the hospital and into a family room. I kept thinking about Letisha's mum. Her daughter was supposed to be sleeping over at my house that night. She wasn't expecting her home so unless somebody had called to tell her what had happened she wouldn't know anything was wrong.

I was in shock, but I didn't have any idea just how serious it was. A couple of weeks earlier a girl from Wheeler Street had been shot in the leg while out at a club. I didn't know the girl who was shot but it happened on my road, in front of my house. I couldn't believe something like that could happen on my street, so when it did I immediately thought my daughters would have the same injuries as that other girl – a shot in the leg or the hand, something like that.

After about half an hour a doctor and a police officer came into the room and sat down. I knew then it was bad news. They told me what had happened. I don't know how they are supposed to tell people things like this. I don't know if it's just how they do it or if it's because I didn't expect them to say what they did, but their words came across to me cold. That same doctor and police officer had to deliver the news twice that night because first they told me and then Letisha's mum arrived at the hospital.

I don't like to think of the words I heard in that room, but the gist of it was that Charlene was dead and Sophie was in a critical condition and had suffered several bullet wounds. I was asked if I wanted to see her. I still couldn't comprehend what had happened. I thought that somebody had gone up to the two of them and shot repeatedly. I imagined the weapon being a hand gun. I never thought anyone could be on the streets of Birmingham carrying a MAC-10 machine gun. I went to the room where Sophie was but all I could see was blood. I couldn't make myself step through the door, so I didn't go up to her. Instead I stood in the doorway in disbelief.

I was told that I had to identify Charlene's body. I said I didn't want to because I didn't want that image of her in my mind. I was very clear about that, but their response was equally firm. I had no choice. It took a long time for them to get me to the mortuary, but I had to identify Charlene's body, and in the end I did.

When I got home the shooting was on the television news. As soon as I saw the bullet holes in the wall I could understand why some survived and others didn't.

Sophie had to undergo a number of operations and was in hospital for weeks afterwards. She still has scars and nerve damage caused by the bullet wounds. It was more than two years before the four young men involved were found guilty of the murders and each jailed for a minimum of 35 years. One of the four convicted was Sophie and Charlene's half-brother, Marcus Ellis, and the newspaper headlines read, 'Brother shot sister'. Walking along the road I felt that everyone was looking at me because my photo had been all over the press and I didn't know if they were looking at me thinking, she's the woman who lost her daughter or, she's the woman whose son shot her daughter. The thought of people thinking it was my son who did this was an extra weight to carry. He wasn't my son. I didn't even know the boy.

Following the court case, the editor of the Birmingham Evening Mail approached me and said that the paper would like to do something in memory of the two girls. He suggested setting up a charity and had the idea for the education awards, because the girls were in education when it happened. I was happy for that to happen because it seemed like a way I could do something good in their names, like there was something positive coming out of something bad. When we first started the education awards it was targeted at university study for people under 30 years old. When I met these people, while I was glad to help them, I felt they were already high achievers to have got so far and maybe we should try to do something for underprivileged people who hadn't yet got to that stage in their education. So that's what we did. At the same time we broadened our reach geographically and in terms of age range, offering the awards to anyone aged 16 or over, because I felt that there are lots of people over 30 years old who would like to get back into education but don't have the opportunity to.

Once we made that change we had a much bigger mix of people coming through the door and it wasn't long before I found myself face-to-face with a former gang member. It wasn't something I would have chosen to do, but in the interview situation I began to think, okay maybe he wants to do better now and change his life. In many ways he had changed already and wanted an education. I thought – let's give him a chance to change for the better, and from that meeting I started to think that perhaps I could help to change people's lives, and the knock-on effect would benefit other people's lives.

David Blunkett, who was Home Secretary at the time, set up an All-Party Parliamentary Group on Gun Crime and I was invited to speak. My view was that you can't just work with an individual because if a child is problematic you've got to work out where the problem is coming from. Most work at that time was being done with the difficult person in a family. My thought was, it's great to help an individual but what about the rest of the family?

The first families I worked with I met through the police. Most of these families were anti-police and after a few visits I started thinking that perhaps some of that antagonism came because the police were saying things that the families didn't want to hear. I was pleased to do that work because I had a message to give to mums of those boys that I hoped could change lives. If their son is living that way there are only three roads he can go down and none are to a good place. He could get locked up, she could bury her son, or her son could harm someone else. It's not something people want to hear, but they need to know.

One lady told me, 'I don't want to speak to nobody.'

I said: 'I know you told the police that, but if I speak to you for five minutes and you feel like you want to stop at five minutes, then you can stop and say I don't want to speak any more.'

She started speaking. Five minutes passed, then ten, half an hour, one hour. I said, 'Do you want to stop?'

'No', she said and carried on. That was how I got through to her.

The men who shot my daughters were enacting a revenge attack for a shooting that had happened some weeks before. It was a botched attack from one gang member on a rival gang member and my daughters were innocent bystanders caught up in the violence. It was some years later when the police asked if Sophie and I would meet a girl who had been jailed for her part in the earlier shooting. The idea was for us to work together to explain to people about the often tragic consequences of getting involved with gangs. Sophie said no, but because the police said that this girl was remorseful, although it was difficult for me to go to see her, I agreed. When we met, the girl came across as if the time she spent in prison had changed her, so I asked Sophie if she would visit her too. This time she agreed and when the two met Sophie said that she felt the girl wanted to give back in some way, so if it could help other people, she would work with her.

That's how we started Pandora's Box. It's a workshop that shows how one person's actions can affect other people's lives – people they don't know, in ways they don't know. The former gang member tells her story. Her story had an impact on Sophie's life, so then Sophie tells her story and because what happened to her had an impact on me, I then tell my story. I find it hard to talk about what happened, but telling it in this way I feel I am impacting on other people's lives and they appreciate it.

Recently Sophie and I took part in a workshop at a lifers' prison. When we finished talking all these prisoners came up to speak to us. They wanted to ask us questions and tell us about what they had done that had caused them to be imprisoned. One of them was crying. He said: 'I've never heard a victim speak before. Now I know what I've done.' That was him speaking behind locked doors. Would he have said it outside? I don't know, but it felt that there was some realisation of what he'd done and how he'd hurt the family of his victim. For us, even if just one person receives our message, it has been worth it.

I've met lots of parents who have lost their children in violent ways and the pain doesn't go away. I can never move on from what has happened to my family, but through these interactions I am trying to do something for the better.

6   Calls to My Sister

Mary Kolu Massaquoi

Mary Kolu Massaquoi is the creator of a radio show, Calls to My Sister, which uses drama to convey health messages to audiences on the African continent. Mary, a former nurse and midwife who recently retrained in nutrition and public health, uses her experience of growing up in Liberia and later working in a hospital during the country's civil war to share essential advice in an accessible way. During the 2014 outbreak of Ebola virus disease in West Africa, Mary produced five emergency response programmes and was later invited to help shape a new BBC Media Action radio drama, to improve knowledge about the virus.

> **'You will know them by their fruits. Are grapes gathered from thorns, or figs from thistles?'**
> **(Matthew 7:16).**

John Sentamu writes:

In the garden at Bishopthorpe Palace we have some very special fruit trees – two figs and two mulberry trees – which Archbishop Desmond Tutu and I planted when he visited in the autumn of 2013.

These are very long-lived trees and, as we planted them, we thought of the fruit that we and others after us, would enjoy as they grew and matured.

Jesus told his followers that people would know what kind of people they were from the fruits their lives displayed. We do not expect our fig trees or our mulberry trees to produce lemons or aloes; no, we hope they will produce the loveliest and tastiest figs and mulberries possible.

Mary Kolu's life journey has taken her to many different places. She was transplanted and grafted into new situations, but the true fruit of her life grown in God's love was seen in everything she did. Fruit which brought refreshment and delight for those around her. Like the fig and the mulberry, Mary Kolu is a long-lived source of fruit and blessing. May we all show the fruit of God's grace throughout our lives. Fruit grown in us by the Holy Spirit: **'Love, joy, peace, patience, kindness, generosity, faithfulness, gentleness, and self-control'** (Galatians 5:22).

☩

It's only with hindsight that we can see how one experience in life opens doors to another, sometimes many years later. I was in my sixth decade when I produced the radio programme, *Calls to My Sister*. My birth place, my ancestry, my work and life experience all contributed to my having the idea and making it work. When something like that happens you realise no experience in life is wasted, you never know when or how the Lord might use it for good.

I was born in Zorzor, a small village in Liberia close to the Guinea border more than 7,000km from where I now call home in Bradford, England. I was the first child in a family of nine; four girls and five boys. After I was born my father travelled south of the country for work and my mother joined him, leaving me in the care of my grandparents in the nearby villages of Sucromu and Kiliwu. When I was seven years old my parents returned to take me to school, a two-hour drive away in Salayea, where I stayed with one of my father's distant relatives, who was a teacher for the Lutheran mission. My dad's relative and his wife were good people, but their home, being a secluded house, with a valley separating them from the main village, was the opposite of what I'd grown used to. Until then I'd always lived surrounded by aunts, uncles and cousins. Lonely and homesick I cried so much that eventually my father's relative took me back to Sucromo.

Coincidentally for me, the Lutheran mission school had recently started up in the village. Our classes were in a hut to begin with, but there were plans for a proper school, and later my cousins and I helped collect sand from the riverside to make the bricks from which our school was built. I spent three happy years at that school before it was time to move on again. By this time my father was working as an apprentice auto mechanic for the Liberia Iron Ore Mining Company in Bomi Hills, where I joined another mission school to continue my education, after which I was blessed to win a scholarship to the Rick Institute Senior High boarding school. Sharing a room with 11 other girls reminded me of my childhood growing up in the villages. During term-time I helped the school nurse for an hour a day, for which I was paid. I enjoyed the work as well as the extra pocket change so when I got an opportunity, through my father's employer, to work in a hospital during the holidays I jumped at it. I held the idea that my grandmother, my father's mother, would like me to work as a nurse, and although I could never recall the conversation when she said that, the thought was always in the back of my mind.

Once I had my senior secondary school certificate, more opportunities opened up to me and I was given the option to study nursing at home in Liberia or in England, where the head of the hospital, Dr Rupert Prescott was from. I liked Dr and Mrs Prescott and the idea of travelling to see them in their home country was exciting, but there was also a more pressing reason why studying in England appealed to me. If I stayed in Liberia I knew the pressure from my family for me to marry would be too strong to resist, and I would be unable to continue my studies. At the time I was engaged to be married, through no choice of my own, to a man I didn't love. I knew that if I moved to England there was a chance he would find someone else and I would be free.

My first few weeks in England were spent with Dr Prescott and his family in the Yorkshire town of Hessle while I waited for the nursing school in Leeds to open for a new intake. Dr and Mrs Prescott had twin children living at home, who were four years younger than me, and Mrs Prescott's parents lived in the flat upstairs. In the evenings everyone ate dinner together and being part of an extended family was wonderful, because it was like home-from-home for me. Mrs Prescott helped me to pick out something suitable to wear because, as I soon learned, my Liberian clothing was in no way suited to a British winter. Of course, the weather wasn't the only thing that took some getting used to. In Liberia at that time everything I ate was either harvested or caught in the river that day. I never stored food, so when I opened the kitchen cupboards and saw all these tins and jars, at first I thought it was a shop and that the Prescotts must be selling food on the side! There was a lot to learn about the English way of life, particularly the amount of documentation there was to deal with. People would say, 'Have you filled in this form?' and I'd think, I must have done because I've filled in so many. I'd then find out that there was yet another one to be completed – in my whole life I'd never filled in so many forms!

When I went to enrol at the college there were two levels of nursing training. Mrs Prescott, who knew me, thought that I should do the higher registered training but Leeds Infirmary questioned my qualifications and I was told to sign-up for a second level, enrolled nurse. I was gutted at this decision, but also determined that at some point I would complete my registered training. So, after two years practical training to qualify as an enrolled nurse I applied again, this time to Bradford, where at the interview I was told: 'We will take you because Dr Prescott said you are determined to do this and you're not going to stop until you do it.' He was right. After I got that qualification I continued my nursing training in midwifery and tropical diseases. I'd got a thirst for learning, so when a minister in my church suggested that I do radio training, I decided to follow his advice and see what opportunities were available, even though I couldn't see when I might use it.

In 1986, 14 years after I came to the UK, I returned to Liberia to work at ELWA Mission Hospital, where I had a job on the wards as well as teaching in Monrovia Bible College across the road, where I taught basic health information to pastors who might be placed in a village without access to medical facilities. My role at ELWA was initially for a year, but that job led to another in the centre of the country, which was where I was when the civil war came.

War broke out in the north of the country on Christmas Eve 1989. I had the opportunity to leave, but the call came while I was on duty at the hospital and I felt strongly that I should stay. Our 30-bed children's ward was suddenly packed with more than 60 children, many of whom were from the front-line. Some were fighters' children and other children from the war front; many were malnourished and diseased. Some hardly 10 years old, who had been unlawfully recruited and given automatic weapons to wreak terror on communities, were nursed in the adult ward adjacent to the younger children. They often regretted destroying the medications in hospitals, as we too were very short of pain relief for the same reason.

I managed to escape the war a year later, crossing the border as a refugee to the Ivory Coast. For the next six months I worked voluntarily for the United Nations, and with no sign of the war ending I came back to England, the only other place I knew as home. It was another two decades before peace finally came to my country and I haven't been able to return since.

Some years later I stopped nursing, due to ill health, and began working with my church to support homeless people in the area. It was through this work that I was invited to attend a lecture on healthy living. I was interested to go along initially because I knew that lifestyle changes and nutrition could have a positive impact on my health and wanted to find out more. When the lecturer found out that I was a midwife he encouraged me to do a degree in health, wellbeing and social care. I wasn't sure if I would be able to, but with his help I applied and was accepted. I soon realised the course wasn't for me, and fortunately was able to transfer to a nutrition and public health degree at Huddersfield University and this time I knew I'd made the right choice.

Calls to My Sister grew out of a work placement I did as part of my university course, although in reality it felt as if the seeds were sown many years before. For my placement I returned to Radio Worldwide, where I had done some training all those years before. The station was now based in Leeds and was working with a missionary body, Reach Beyond, with links to several radio stations in Africa. Every week I call my sister Gomah in Liberia. Often things would come up in conversation and I'd find myself naturally offering advice about health and I wondered if we might use the radio to communicate important health messages in the same kind of way.

We decided to produce a number of short two to three minute programmes, based around the concept of a phone call to my sister with nuggets of information on health, hygiene and nutrition slipped into the conversation. I'd cover universally important topics such as hand washing, but also issues that were specifically important to an African audience, particularly sensitive issues that many people don't talk about. For example, there is a belief held by many women in Liberia and other African countries that when breastfeeding a woman must not sleep with her husband in case his semen contaminates the breast milk and makes the baby seriously ill. Traditionally in Liberia, women breastfeed their daughters for three years and their sons for four years. Sometimes my mum would help my aunties by feeding their babies rice water. Looking back, it was perhaps because my aunts slept with their husbands and so refrained from giving breast milk to the babies, in case the babies became get sick and died. It wasn't true, of course, but that belief was depriving babies of breast milk and so contributing to child malnutrition. A man who went to school and learned biology knew this belief about semen contaminating breast milk wasn't true, so he would want to sleep with his wife and encourage her to go ahead, but a woman who had no education couldn't have that on her conscience and would choose to stop breastfeeding instead. This was the group of women I was hoping to reach through my programme – women who were intelligent but who had little or no education, couldn't read or write and were therefore unable to access important health information in other ways.

The programmes were recorded at a studio in Bradford. Although I knew they were being aired across Sub-Saharan Africa the reality of that only hit me when on a call home, Gomah held the phone to her radio and said: 'Listen, it's your programme'. I was pleasantly surprised! My radio programme, airing through my sister's kitchen as clear as if I was there talking to her myself. 'It's generated a lot of interest,' she said. 'Everyone wants to listen to it.' According to Gomah, *Calls to My Sister* was doing exactly what we had set out to do, dispensing the kind of information people need in a way they could understand. I later found out from a radio station in River Cess, Liberia that even the Chief of the township had noticed a change in people's behaviour in the community. People were making healthier choices but there was a knock-on effect we hadn't considered – people weren't visiting the hospital as much, purely for health advice, because they were getting this advice elsewhere, leaving the hospital staff with more time to deal with sick patients most in need of their help.

During my placement year I produced 26 episodes of *Calls to my Sister*. After graduation, I began working on a new series of broadcasts, this time dealing with the 2014 Ebola virus disease outbreak in West Africa. From speaking to my sister, as well as healthcare workers, government officials, media personnel, and World Health Organization sources, I knew that there was a lot of fear and misinformation hampering efforts to tackle the outbreak. In some areas there was a belief that any outsider could carry the infection, which was leading terrified villagers, in some remote areas, to kill health workers who were coming in to help. I wanted to put together some essential advice based on what we did know about preventing the spread of disease, such as hygiene and isolating people with symptoms. I wanted to help save lives by spreading accurate messages about the Ebola virus disease; messages that local people could trust and understand, and that would help to curb the spread of rumours and false information.

During the 2014 outbreak we produced five emergency response programmes covering topics such as hygiene and the importance of isolating people with symptoms. The programmes came to the attention of BBC Media Action – the corporation's international development arm – and I was approached to help develop a series of programmes under the title, Kick Ebola from Liberia, with a similar aim of spreading important messages in a dramatic format, to enable the audience to hear information in a conversational way that addressed their concerns.

In January 2016 the World Health Organization declared Liberia to be Ebola free. I don't know what part my programmes played in that, but I do know that rumours and misinformation put everybody at risk and that good communication is essential to tackle any major health problem. To be able to play even a small part in that was amazing and something I never could have imagined. I still make programmes in the *Calls to My Sister* series and I've recently been invited to work on a new programme called *Senior Moments* for Bradford Community Broadcasting. I'd never thought of myself as a senior person, but at 64 years old I suppose I am. Now I think – how wonderful, that God is already using this phase of my life in new and exciting ways.

7 Find the treasure

Claire Daniels

Claire Daniels runs the Rainbow Money project in Scarborough which provides a vital life-line to community members struggling with debt. She is also an advocate for Acts 435, a website managed through a network of churches and local charities, which allows people to give money directly to support a specific request for help from a person in need.

**'Do not judge, so that you may not be judged'.
(Matt. 7:1)**

John Sentamu writes:

My mother often used to say – always be careful when you point a finger at others – because you'll see that three fingers are pointing back at you!

We live in a hypercritical society. Game shows encourage us to judge and vote on people's worth; some chat shows encourage the audience to shout criticisms at the participants. If we find we're being *hyper*critical, we must check to see whether in fact we're being hypocritical! Play-acting.

Jesus warned his followers about hasty and unthinking criticism of others when he says: **'How can you see clearly to take a speck out of your brother's eye, when there is a great plank in your own?'** (Matthew 7:3-5)

Claire discovered that, like many of us, her attitude to those in debt had been judgemental. But God led her into a way in which she could understand their problems. At the same time he showed her that she had her own weakness – a compulsion for overwork leading to stress. We all need to learn, by the power of the Holy Spirit, humility and self-knowledge as we look to help others. Jesus Christ alone is entitled to judge, because **'only he is gentle and humble in heart'** (Matthew 11:29), has enough love. If we can learn to love like him, then we, like Claire, can truly be of service to others.

✝

Behind every story is a set of circumstances we know little or nothing about. We can try to put ourselves in that same situation and ask: how could that have happened? What would we have done or how might we have felt? However, the first step to truly understanding another person is to listen. I'd say that is the big part of what I do.

I've always been open to the idea that people's lives aren't straightforward, but even so, if years ago you had asked me why the majority of people are in debt, I would have said, because they are or have been irresponsible with money. If you did a straw poll I'm sure the majority of people still think that way, but after hearing the stories of hundreds of people struggling with debt, I'd say less than five per cent are in this situation because of frivolous spending or mismanagement of money. Could we live on £73.10 a week? People I work with who are, and who aren't getting into any more debt, are my heroes. How they are doing it, I don't know. For most people in debt, an unfortunate circumstance has caused them to be in that situation and sadly they can experience so much judgement for it.

I don't pretend I know first-hand what it is like to live life on the bread line. Everyone has problems, but in terms of finances I've been lucky in so far as I've never had serious money worries. Being unable to meet the repayments on our car loan was the nearest I came to experiencing what it was like to find myself in debt. Thankfully the problem was a short-lived because someone stepped in and bailed us out, but what if they hadn't?

That experience on its own didn't help me to see debt differently. In many ways I stumbled into debt advice. I was working for N:qu?re, an advice, information and support service I'd set up through the community café attached to our church in Reading. On the estate where we lived many people were frustrated at being unable to access the state benefits they were entitled to. The main obstacle for them seemed to be how to fill in the relevant forms and I thought I could probably help with that.

Initially my focus was on form-filling, but once people started to open up about their financial circumstances I began to see just how much of a problem debt had become for many people on the estate. It was shocking to me just how much debt people could accumulate in such a short time. Many of the stories were heartbreaking and I was hearing them from people of all ages and from all walks of life. I came across lots of elderly people who had lost money through scam competitions. We are more familiar with such scams these days – vulnerable people receive a letter through the post telling them that they've won a large amount of money, all they need to do to claim the prize is enter a competition, dial a premium phone number, send off £15 – you know the rest. A lot more people than you might imagine got caught out by frauds like these, and often through embarrassment or shame didn't want to admit the money problems they'd got into because of it.

At times I wondered how on earth I could help these people. My instinct is to be a fixer, to do what I can to make things better. Unfortunately that often led me to take other people's stress onto myself as if it was my own. I was 25 years old and believed that I was going to save the world. I'd take work home, but however much I did it was never enough, there was always more to do.

I learned to give things to God through burnout. Working at the centre was incredibly fruitful in seeing lives changed, but the stress of running such a high intensity project alone, while caring for two children at home took its toll. After five full-on years I got to a place where I couldn't cope anymore. I was totally overwhelmed and unable to face things that before I would have taken in my stride. If someone else was looking in on my life they might have said, okay why don't you do, A, B, C, D and E, and it'll be fine, but you can't see that when you're heading towards burnout – there seems no way forward, no way out. After a week-long hospital stay it was clear to everyone around me that I wasn't managing at all. At that point, I knew I had to leave so reluctantly, I did.

I took an accounts job, which was largely screen work with little contact with people. I began doing a little pastoral work in the church but I realised that to stay well I needed to change the way I did things. I could still think: how can I make this situation better or how can I make this person feel better? The change was not getting frantic about it.

Praise God, N:qu?re is now 15 years old and still going strong. It is better than it ever was and I've grown too in that time. After I left, two people were employed to do the work I'd been doing on my own for years. That was another wake-up call. Perhaps I could have asked for help. Whatever else, I couldn't let myself get into that situation again.

Looking for a change, my family moved north and we spent some time in Bridlington. It's a quiet seaside town where there are no motorways within 40 miles, and you can get across town with ease at any time of day because there is no rush hour. The place was everything I needed and helped me to restore my energy and my health.

I've come to realise that nobody can fix somebody else's life, only Jesus can do that. All I can do is to play my part and when I'm doing well, that's where I am. I've given that person to God. I'm doing my bit in being obedient and I'll do my part in whatever God wants me to do, but I won't try to fix everything. If I find that I've started thinking that I can fix people, that's usually when things start to go wrong. It's like I've stepped out of my remit, I've left God out of the picture and everything goes pear-shaped.

When a job opening came up for a debt advice coordinator at the Rainbow Centre I started to feel excited about work again. Initially I had a slight reservation because of how quickly I'd reached burnout managing a project on my own back in Reading. This would be different though because I wouldn't be working on my own. The Rainbow Centre is affiliated to Community Money Advice, a national organisation that enables and supports local churches and community groups to set up debt advice provision in their area. I would have a manager and CEO at Rainbow Money as well as support from the affiliate organisation. I felt like the job had been made for me.

I've always been honest about where I've failed in the past so people are aware of my weaknesses. Thankfully I've got good, supportive management at the centre and people around who'll say turn your phone off, stop taking calls outside of work time, stop doing so many voluntary hours and go home. Hearing those things from people who care really helps. For my part, I've also helped myself by learning to trust God more. The debt service isn't mine, even if in one sense I have taken it from scratch and built it into what it is, it's still not mine, it belongs to God. I'm not indispensable and part of recognising that comes with maturity, thinking, okay, this is what God has called me to do for a season with these people, I can do my part and I need to trust God with the rest. I know when I'm doing that well, because I'm giving what I do to God, letting him be in control of it and recognising that I'm not there to fix people's lives.

These are all things that I've learned over time and it's about making those lessons work practically, and having the wisdom to know when to go home and when it is important to respond immediately. I can't be there for people night and day, but at the same time I'm not so fixed that I can't reply to someone at eight o'clock in the evening if it's appropriate, so that they can get a good night's sleep, rather than my leaving it until ten o'clock the next morning and having them tossing and turning with anxiety all night. An important part of what we do is being there for people, being a listening ear, someone to come to without always having to wait for a designated appointment.

People want and need to feel listened to. Even if I've done nothing else, the fact that I've taken their paperwork, I've listened and I've said there is an answer, that's enough for them to begin to feel better. There is always an answer and lots of people are unaware that they don't need to pay for that answer. There are not-for-profit debt advice services, like ours, all across the country where they can turn for help.

Many people who get into debt panic. They are terrified that their children will be taken away, that they'll be sent to prison, or that bailiffs will show up and take all their belongings. There is a lot of misinformation around and providing a few legal facts can be a massive help. It's also important to help people out of the blame game. It's not always someone's fault. In recent years I've taken several publicans through full bankruptcy. Lots of pubs are failing in Scarborough, and while it doesn't make it easier to know that, there is some comfort in knowing that they are not alone in this situation and what is happening is not their fault.

There is always an expectation when people come for advice that they are going to be judged for their situation. It's very important to take away that sense of failure and fault, and instead to focus on the good things, things people have done well. Guilt and shame starts to evaporate when someone gives you hope. Showing people where they are doing well with their budgeting sometimes motivates them to want to do better. The key for me is to find the treasure – what's good that I can pull out? Most of the time there is something, even if it is simply that they've made it to the appointment – they are here, sitting in front of me. I don't do many home visits, unless someone is disabled and finds it difficult to travel. The fact that a person has come in shows some responsibility because a lot of people don't show up. I can say: you've made it; you're here. Now things can start to improve. It's the same for all of us in life. If someone says we're doing something wrong it often makes things worse, but when someone points out what we're doing well it pushes us to want to do better.

My job is to be the middle-man by negotiating with creditors to find a solution. That one act can take a lot of stress off people. It's never the same dealing with your own problems. Even people who are fantastic at dealing with other people's problems professionally can find their own problems overwhelming. Sometimes something as simple as saying, 'I'll take it, I'll deal with it', can take a huge weight off. We've got the power of headed paper, which works wonders too.

Being an advocate for Acts 435 gives me an extra tool to be able to say let's see if we can meet one of your needs. The charity is inspired by the works of the early church, as described in Acts 4:32 to 4:35, where the early disciples share their possessions, and pass money to the apostles to give to anyone in need. The charity works by matching up those who want to give with those in need. Requests are anonymised and all the money collected goes straight to the individual it was donated to help. Sometimes we use the charity to raise money for practical needs such as purchasing household items like cookers and fridges. We've also raised funds for a lot of debt relief orders this way. It may seem strange to ask for donations to help get someone through insolvency, but for some people finding the £90 to be able to do that is overwhelming. For some people, who may not have paid a bill for three years, insolvency is the chance for a fresh start and has motivated them to start budgeting and look at their finances in a completely different way.

I have helped more than 700 clients through their debt issues and have made over 100 successful applications through Acts 435. All those lives have been changed for the better and it is an amazing privilege to be part of their journey. The satisfaction of working in debt advice is like nothing else I've ever done. It enables me to help people so easily – there is a straightforward strategy I can implement and when I'm expressing God's heart in that, there's an extra compassion that often people aren't expecting. It says, I'm listening and I want to do everything I can to help you – knowing that changes people's lives.

8 *Outpouring of love*

Muthoni Kanga

Muthoni Kanga was working for the international relief and development agency, International Aid Services (IAS) in Somalia when her vehicle was ambushed by pirates. Muthoni was kidnapped on 11 July 2012, along with two colleagues, Martin Mutisya Kioko and Abdinoor Dabaso Boru, and held hostage for 694 days. The Aid Worker Security Report lists 167 incidents of major violence against aid workers in 19 countries during 2012. These attacks resulted in 274 aid workers killed, kidnapped, or seriously wounded. Despite these figures increasing in recent years, IAS and other international agencies continue humanitarian work in Somalia and other hostile environments around the world.

'Do not fear, for I am with you, do not be afraid, for I am your God; I will strengthen you, I will help you, I will uphold you with my victorious right hand. For

I, the Lord your God, hold your right hand; it is I who
say to you, 'Do not fear, I will help you'
(Isaiah 41:10, 13).

John Sentamu writes:

Muthoni's story brings to life one of the great fears we have
for those who work or travel in troubled areas of the world.
Piracy is not just an old story of Captain Hook or Captain
Jack Sparrow, it is a brutal reality of people preying on others
– often on people who are trying to bring help and blessing to
the countries where it happens.

But as Muthoni found, God did not leave her helpless for
ever. He kept his promise to strengthen her and help her until
she was returned to her colleagues and family. And he is still
strengthening her now as she continues to recover and move
on.

Many of us have to deal with threatening and fearful
situations in our lives – even if they are not as dangerous as
that suffered by Muthoni. But God's promises can always
be relied on. He knows that we will often be afraid and he is
always ready to comfort and reassure us.

There are seventy-five verses in the Revised Standard
Version of the Bible where God says to his people – and to us -
'Do not be afraid'. Let us then not fear, because he will always
be faithful to help us. And let us remember that *'There is no*
fear in love, but perfect love casts out fear; for fear has to
do with punishment, and whoever fears has not yet reached
perfection in love. We love because he first loved us' (1 John
4:18-19).

✠

My job has taken me into many hostile environments,
where situations can suddenly change drastically. In the two
years before the attack I had visited the Puntland region of
Somalia many times. We were working on a project to

improve water supplies in the region, which included building physical structures such as water collection points, shallow wells, reservoirs and latrines. Part of our task that week was to supervise the completion of the work and part of it was to reach out to people in the more remote villages and communities, collecting case studies so that we could develop further work to best reflect local needs.

We'd arrived from Nairobi on the Monday and found accommodation at a guest house in the town, which we used as our base. On Tuesday we did a full day's work as normal. We travelled in a convoy protected by armed guards, but that was a security requirement of us working in that area and was not unusual. On Wednesday we drove away from the town for about five hours and after a full day's work we said goodbye to the people we'd met in the community. At about 5.30pm we began our journey back to the town. We were not ten minutes into that journey when a vehicle appeared from the thorn thickets and stopped in front of our convoy blocking the road.

I'd never witnessed anything like this. I knew something bad was happening, but I didn't know what. I thought perhaps they were robbers. I heard a gunshot but I couldn't see who was shooting. The armed escort travelling with us overtook our vehicle and I saw the passengers from both vehicles jump out and start talking. The policemen travelling with us were challenging whoever these people were, but it soon became clear that our guards were both out-manned and out-armed. The police officers' AK-47s were no match for the gang's machine guns. Panicked, our driver slammed our vehicle in reverse and began a getaway. We didn't get very far because the gang opened fire. There was a spray of bullets, the tyres on the vehicle deflated. Our driver was unhurt and escaped on foot, but his co-driver, our local Somali liaison officer who was also sat in the front, was badly wounded. I couldn't see him from where I was but another colleague could see how bad his injuries were and shouted for us to get out of the vehicle. We opened the doors and ran.

The surrounding area is mostly shrub land and thorny bushes. There was nowhere to hide and we didn't get very far, maybe a few metres, before we realised there were men in front of us and behind – we were surrounded. They began circling us and firing guns in the air. We surrendered and the pirates threw us in the back of a vehicle where I passed out. When I came round I could still hear gun shots and fast braking. It was another 24 hours before I realised that I was bleeding from shrapnel wounds to my scalp and left shoulder.

By this time the sun was coming down so most of our travel was in the dark. Everything we were carrying such as our travel and identification documents, phones and money were taken from us. The pirates were asking us lots of questions. I think they had assumed wrongly that we worked for the United Nations. At one point we had to abandon the vehicle we were travelling in because the tyres kept deflating. Once we had a new vehicle we drove for many hours through the night, stopping only once for a toilet break and to send for supplies from a village along the way. I remember we were each given a bottle of water, but we didn't get any cooked food until the next evening. I remember that one of the pirates gave me his jacket to wear. I wasn't cold, but I was terrified and did whatever I was told, so I just took it and put it on.

For almost two years after that we lived in the Somalian bush, away from villages and any passing traffic. The only people who came into view were herders and whenever that happened guards fired shots into the air to warn them off. In my opinion there was no way we could have escaped. So as to go unnoticed we were often on the move and our camps were makeshift – a shack put together with branches, twigs and a couple of poles. Sometimes, if we were lucky, we were given a plastic sheet which we put under the branches to help keep out the rain and we used anything we could collect to protect us from extreme wind and sun.

Our daily routine varied depending on the season and if we were moving camp. Most days I would wake with the sunrise, which was usually about 6am, sometimes earlier. I would always try to use that time for early morning prayers, quiet reflection and meditation. After that we waited for breakfast which was our main activity until we were brought dinner at 6pm. Once in a while we were brought some very sweet black tea to drink, but for the most part we sat for hours staring into the open space.

To keep our minds occupied the three of us would tell stories. We'd talk about things that had happened in our lives and what we hoped to do when we were back home, but after a year we found that we were telling the same stories over and over again. Twice we were given a tiny short-wave radio, which the guards demanded we share with them. The radios each lasted for about four to six months before breaking down, but the times we were allowed to listen to it were our best moments. We listened to Vatican radio and the BBC and would talk about the issues we had heard – it gave us fresh stories to talk about and a hope of something outside of the life we'd come to know.

I tried, as far as possible, to put my situation in context of other human suffering and there was much worse suffering in the world than we were going through. On the BBC radio we would hear brilliant stories of people's experiences, some of them were hostages, and I would remind myself that we weren't alone in our pain.

The same men guarded us for the whole hostage period. Once in a while one of my colleagues, who is from a similar culture to the Somalis, would play cards with them. My other colleague kept away from the guards as much as possible and I, being a woman, was only allowed by the local culture, religion and sensibilities to have necessary contact with the male guards.

In the early days of our capture I did wonder why God was allowing me to go through this ordeal; what I had done to deserve it and why I was being punished. As time went on those thoughts left me because I knew with every day that went by I was only surviving because of the strength God was giving me to survive – I was so tired and fed-up, I didn't have any strength or will to do it myself. I felt that God used opportunities every day to assure me of his presence – through nature, birds and animals. Whenever camels stayed by our shelter all day or I'd see a bright rainbow overhead, I'd take those as beautiful signs that God cared for me. I'd remind myself about what God says about us in his word, about his plans for our future. When birds began perching on our shelter every morning I heard their song as God saying to me, 'You have the victory.' That thought kept me hanging in there, although I didn't know if I was hanging in to get out alive, or if I was hanging in to live for one more day.

I prayed with my whole heart that we would be released, that I'd get a second chance to be at home with my family and friends and to come back to my life. In all honesty I didn't know how it would end, if we would be released or if pirates were going to kill us. We knew that there were negotiations taking place, although we didn't know what these were. Sometimes we would hear the guards talking about different options and the option to kill us was always considered. I realised that the more I thought about how it all might end the less strength I had to keep going, so I didn't think about it. Instead I'd try to think about my immediate needs, one day at a time – simple things like, did I have enough water for the day, how could I patch up my worn clothes, and if the guard on duty was friendly enough for me to request favours such as soap, a comb or medicine.

On several occasions we were allowed to speak to our families on the telephone. The first time was sudden and unexpected. We were given two minutes to tell our families that we were alive and well. I had never imagined we would get to do that and it was such a relief. The later phone calls were distressing because we had to persuade our families to put pressure on the organisations the pirates were negotiating with and we were told what we had to say. Sometimes, when I got a chance to speak to my family I would use my mother tongue because there were things I needed to say that I didn't want the guards to hear. Thankfully they didn't care and I took this as a sign of God's grace also.

We were informed of our release by professional negotiators who told us that a consensus had been reached with our captors. At the time we weren't sure what to believe. We'd had our hopes dashed before, although this time was different. The message was coming from Nairobi and previous times the same message had always come from within the gang. It was about ten days, maybe more, after this call that our lead guard told us one morning after breakfast to pack our things because we were going somewhere. As we started to pack up our blankets and things for the camp he said: 'Just take the water.' We were put in two vehicles and did not know where we were headed. It was a hair-raising journey because the guards were incredibly tense. We were driving through the bush, but along tracks that other vehicles could use as well. Twice other vehicles were spotted in the distance and both times we stopped while the pirates took a defensive stance to attack the vehicle should it come our way. About three hours later we stopped in what seemed like the middle of nowhere. There were three other vehicles and I recognised leaders of other gangs. I was told to get out and as I stepped down I saw two of my colleagues from the organisation – they had come to take us home! One of them rushed to me and I hugged him and broke down in tears. 'Where are the others?' he asked. I pointed; they were still in the vehicle. After all the tension and hostility of the morning, although the pirates were still armed, the actual exchange felt very cordial. We got into another vehicle with our colleagues, the pirates got back into their vehicle and we drove off in opposite directions.

It was a four hour drive to the city of Galcayo where we checked into the hotel we stayed in whilst flights were arranged to take us home. For the first time in almost two years I was able to shower, to eat normal food and to lie in a bed. How I had missed those things I'd so often taken for granted.

We were released on a Thursday afternoon and came back to Nairobi on the following Saturday to see our friends and family. For the first month we weren't allowed to meet with crowds of people. There were debriefings and medicals.

The restricted diet I'd been living on meant that I had some problems when I started eating a wider variety of foods again. There are still some issues being sorted out with my bones and teeth, because of a lack of calcium while I was held hostage and also because we were sitting for very long periods without any back rests.

There was so much good will from my family, friends and the church to help me recover and get back on my feet. Gradually I started getting back into everyday activities like going to the bank to reactivate my account, going to Sunday service, travelling on public transport and finding the courage to drive again in the street. I found out that our colleague who was wounded on that day was still alive. The gang had left him for dead and he was rushed to hospital in Nairobi for treatment. He was in a coma for many days and in hospital for three months, but thankfully he survived.

I found out too that prayers had been said for us all over the world. I had notes from the UK, New Zealand, Kenya, Sweden, South Africa, and America – all these people who had been praying for us and all the masses said on our behalf. I believe those prayers built a strong hedge of protection around us so that we weren't destroyed physically, emotionally or spiritually during our ordeal.

Coming home to see the amount of grace and goodwill God has placed in people to help us is overwhelming. Except for us all being in the family of God, these people don't know us and will probably never meet us, yet they took time to hold us in their prayers. I believe it was this outpouring of love that, although we didn't know it at the time, helped to keep our faith and hope alive. Even now when I think about all that love coming our way, it is totally overwhelming.

9   We can be set free

Alan Guile

Professor Alan Guile and his late wife, Betty, began to be asked to pray with people for healing following a weekend retreat in 1973. Eleven years later Alan took early retirement from Leeds University to become available full-time for people to come to their home for inner healing. Since then more than 550 have visited his home in Teesside for prayer to help them to emerge from their past hurts and limitations and gradually reclaim their true selves through the power of God's love.

> **'When the Lord saw that he had turned aside to see, God called to him out of the bush, "Moses, Moses!" And he said, "Here I am." Then he said, "Come no closer! Remove the sandals from your feet, for the place on which you are standing is holy ground"'**
> **(Exodus 3:4-5).**

John Sentamu writes:

The central story of Jewish faith is Exodus. Moses is not a Hebrew name – it is Egyptian – a son of a Hebrew slave raised in Pharaoh's household. He grows up; discovers who he is and has an identity crisis; tries to help the people of his tribe and ends up killing an Egyptian slave-driver; runs away, joins another tribe as a shepherd beyond the desert – he is in uncharted territory. He is not sure who he is but God wants Moses to discover who God wants him to be by revealing to him God's identity as compassion.

So when God's call came to Moses from the midst of the burning bush, Moses was far from ready to take on the task of confronting Pharaoh and leading his people out of exile. He was peacefully looking after his father-in-law's flocks, not looking for a mission. *'Who am I'*, *he said*, *'that I should go… What shall I tell them?'* But God was patient with Moses and provided all the help and strength he needed for this great calling. As he followed and obeyed *'the God of his father, the God of Abraham, the God of Isaac, and the God of Jacob'* (v.6b), and he became a great leader and a man of powerful prayer.

Alan had the same misgivings when he felt he was being led to pray for people's inner healing and restoration. This was an uncomfortable challenge for him at the time, and he has had humbly to be ready to learn new things about himself and others over the decades of prayer that he has been offering. But God is ever ready to teach each one of us and enable us to live out his calling to the full. As Alan says, 'Truly, God picks the most unlikely people.' Moses, Alan, me – and you. We are all called to uncover some of God's purposes. Let us always be ready to listen to God's commanding voice.

✛

I never would have picked myself as a possible candidate for something which involved a great deal of listening. In my younger days I was probably one of the worst listeners anyone could find. When someone spoke to me I would quickly interrupt, afraid that if I waited until they'd finished I might forget what I wanted to say. My mind was so busy working out what my next comment should be that I never properly listened to what the other person had to say. Worse still, when I met someone for the first time, my initial thought would often be: What can this person do for me? Looking back I was an angry person, filled with feelings of inadequacy, with low self-esteem and a debilitating shyness, which led me to avoid much contact with people beyond my immediate family and my work. How did I go from being that man, to being a man who has spent well over 10,000 hours listening to people share the pain and trouble that can rob a human heart of peace and joy? Truly God picks the most unlikely people, in human eyes, because he puts his treasure in earthen vessels in order to show us that it must be his power which is at work.

Looking from the outside you might imagine that I should have been a confident chap – a university professor of electrical engineering; I was married to Betty, who was a good and loving wife, and together we had four children, all in good health. People can carry all kinds of pain that sometimes they don't understand the root of. Many of us are imprisoned by damage from early life which has left us shut-in on ourselves, bound-up with painful feelings and damaged reactions. For 42 years I have been praying with suffering and troubled, but very wonderful people, for their inner healing. For 36 of these years it was in partnership with Betty, my wife of 58 years, and since her death, in 2010, I generally see people on my own. Over the years we prayed with hundreds of people seeking inner healing, including priests, teachers, doctors, psychologists and psychiatrists. I have often been struck by the realisation that when someone reveals to me their hurts and needs, I no longer have the judgemental attitudes I would once have had and might still have even now if I were to read about them in the press rather than meeting them face-to-face. Instead I am aware of being privileged by the person confiding in me and by God allowing me to stand with them 'on holy ground'. I feel compassion and love for them. I'm not on some kind of superior level, but sharing in their brokenness and weakness, like the beggar who says to another, 'I've found a source of good food; if you'd like to walk with me, I'll show you where it is'.

For years I supposed, quite wrongly, that if I were to love and accept myself I would become self-centred. I was in my 60s before it dawned on me that loving and accepting oneself was at one end of a spectrum and being self-centred far away at the other end. It is probably true to say that virtually every one of the many hundreds of people to whom we have listened and with whom we have then prayed, have been, to a greater or lesser degree, unable to love and accept themselves. I was probably in my seventies when I began to fully accept the truth that God loves and accepts me totally as I am, and longs to give the grace for me to love and accept myself. I am now 91 years old and I am still learning.

I can remember the first weekend retreat I went on in 1973, because when Betty and I got there I just wanted to leave and couldn't think why I had thought it might be a good idea to go. Being there made me feel more depressed than when I'd arrived because the more I listened to the other people talking the more inadequate I felt. The other people there seemed to me to be alive in their faith, whereas I felt useless to God and to others. I kept telling myself that I didn't belong, and that someone had made a mistake in inviting us. By the final morning of the retreat this feeling was so strong and painful that I had decided never to risk meeting with others in any prayerful situation ever again. That morning a priest talked to us about waiting on the Lord. I can't say that I remember much of what was said, except that he asked each of us to go away for one hour and pray alone. I'd never prayed for as much as five minutes on my own, but wanting to be obedient I found a hidden spot in a nearby field and tried to pray. I say tried because for the first half-an-hour I was convinced that I wasn't doing it properly, a belief that led me to feel more distressed and unhappy. I was holding a Bible, although, the truth was, I'd never read it. It lived on our bookcase and I suppose I brought it along because I thought other people would have Bibles with them and so bringing one along would be the done thing, as it were. That day as I cried out to God in prayer, I felt the urge to open the Bible and through three passages of Scripture, I had an amazing conversion experience. I knew from that day I was deeply loved by God and that I was beginning a relationship with him through Jesus Christ. That same year Betty experienced a marked deepening of her faith, though her experience was less sudden and dramatic than mine, because unlike me, she had a long, prayerful relationship going back to childhood.

After that Betty and I began to be invited by others to join in praying with people at conferences, days of renewal and retreats, as well as in less formal situations. A few people started coming to our home asking us to pray with them.

Gradually the Lord taught us more about praying for inner healing, often from other people. We have always stressed that people should seek proper medical treatment as well as prayer for healing, and that only a doctor should decide when to stop prescribed medication. What we were gently drawn into was not counselling but listening to the person and to the Holy Spirit, and then praying with them. Two illustrations of the difference suffice. When we attended a 12-day residential course to learn something of counselling, prayer for inner healing and spiritual direction, we had to practise a counselling technique on others. One sister superior said, 'My problem is that I am overburdened and must ask permission of the Order to give up one of my three responsibilities'. The counselling process simply brought tears. When I asked the Lord to reveal the real problem it turned out to be another sister who was always obstructive, not the amount of work. A man who came to see us after attending marriage counselling said: 'They have brought my emotions to the surface but they have left me raw and bleeding'. We were able, as with others, to pray for Jesus to touch the man's wounds with his wounds, and draw out the pain more and more completely into his suffering on the cross.

In 1984, our lives changed again when we both, independently but simultaneously, realised that God was calling us to move to St Joseph's Parish in Stockton-on-Tees. At that time we knew hardly anyone in that area, but because we both felt the same call, we followed it. I gave up my job; we sold our house and bought the bungalow in Norton where I still live. Two years later we were members of a group asked by Bishop Harris of Middlesbrough to work towards building up the healing ministry in his diocese. Gradually our telephone began to ring and someone, recommended by a friend, priest or doctor, would ask if they could come to our home for us to listen to their pain and then pray with them. Within our first year our parish priest commissioned us in the healing ministry, as did a bishop later on. Since then more than 550 people have visited our home for prayer, some travelling hundreds of miles, and from a variety of churches. Out of those, only a couple of people came primarily because of any physical condition.

I am often asked, 'Does it drain you to spend hours listening to people with deep problems?' I can honestly say that neither I nor Betty ever felt drained. Tired? Yes, and often very sad for the people and their circumstances, but we learned to place all the burdens onto Christ. Only Jesus can know intimately the deepest needs of a person, and only he has the power and the love with which to heal them, and is aware of just how difficult it is for someone to open up, and at what pace they are able to go. This takes all pressure off me and I can relax and help them to be as relaxed as it is possible for them to be at each stage of the process. I've learned too from experience that grace always flows both ways, not simply in one direction, and that through this ministry I am being given a wonderful privilege, both by the person trusting me, sometimes telling me things they have never told anyone else, and by God, who allows me to 'stand on holy ground' while he is helping one of his beloved, wounded children.

Betty once said, 'We are all like mummies. We've built up layer upon layer around ourselves and we keep reacting in the same ways because of these layers. Jesus is gradually taking off these layers.' Being God as well as man, and thus outside of time, we can invite him to go back and heal hurts from the past and to release us from burdens of pain locked up in memories in conscious, unconscious or subconscious parts of our mind. Through prayer Jesus can be invited into all our painful memories, particularly from childhood. He can enable the child within us to get in touch with every painful experience and emotion, including those buried or partially buried through our natural defensive reactions, and he can help us to give him permission to begin to dismantle the defensive walls that we built up very early in our lives. Instead of our child-self feeling alone and hopeless, with no one to talk to, understand or help, Jesus can enable our inner child to become aware of his loving presence and to depend on God's protection. Isaiah 53:5 says, by his wounds we are healed. In prayer we invite Jesus to touch the deep wounds in us – all our suffering, anger, resentment, bitterness, lack of forgiveness and disappointment – and let him draw out all the pain into his suffering on the cross. We don't forget our memories but we can be set free from any damage they continue to cause us, so that when we think back to difficult times we no longer flinch or hold onto negative feelings and attitudes.

The Lord wants to reveal more about his ways of healing, but since only he knows the hurts, the needs, and the pace at which each person can proceed, when praying with someone for inner healing we need to be completely dependent on the guidance of the Holy Spirit. I've always stressed that however much we may be allowed to learn about God's way of healing we can never suppose that we are equipped or that we have learnt a method or a technique of going about it. Prayer for inner healing is not a quick fix but a lifetime process in which we learn to depend completely on the Holy Spirit. There is only one healer – Jesus Christ, and through his awesome love he continues to surprise us.

10   Talking about it

Nashipae

Nashipae grew up in a small Maasai village in the Narok County of Kenya where female genital mutilation (FGM) was commonly practised. Although now illegal in many parts of the world, including Kenya, the World Health Organization estimates that in Africa alone there are still three million girls who undergo some form of the procedure every year. Nashipae is using her personal experience to help other women, working as an active campaigner to end FGM and to improve the health and education of girls and women worldwide.

'Speak out for those who cannot speak, for the rights of all the destitute. Speak out, judge righteously, defend the rights of the poor and needy'
(Proverbs 31:8-9).

John Sentamu writes:

Jesus Christ's Galilean springtide manifesto was to *'bring good news to the poor and freedom to the oppressed and to proclaim the year of the Lord's favour'* (Luke 4:18-19). On earth and now in heaven, he is the perfect One who speaks for those who cannot speak, who judges righteously and defends the rights of the needy. His way of doing this was costly. It separated him from family and set those in power against him. But if we are to follow him completely and implicitly, we have to be ready to act in the same way on behalf of those who are unable to act for themselves.

Nashipae's story tells of her struggle, first to come to terms with her own sense of powerlessness against a tradition which gave such pain, and then to come to the conviction that she must speak and act on behalf of others –to bring both comfort and protection.

It is costly to challenge the long-standing traditions of our communities, but in God's strength, Nashipae was able to carry this through. Jesus is always with those who act on behalf of justice for those in need – for that is just what he did for our sakes. His love has brought us everlasting liberty. We are invited to encounter him and bask in his victory.

✝

I was 11 years old when my mother told me: 'It is time for you to become a woman'.

Only minutes earlier I'd been playing outside with my friends and her seriousness took me by surprise. I looked at her, puzzled. 'Mother, what do you mean?'

'I want you to be prepared,' she said and then I realised what she meant. 'You and your sister will become women tomorrow morning.'

That evening there was a huge celebration with lots of food and alcohol. All the attention was on the girls who were to be cut and part of me was excited by it. Our heads were shaved and we were given new clothes to wear and many presents. Some little girls grow up looking forward to this day, a time when they are promised amazing things. They think what is about to happen is a good thing. For me it was different. I was the youngest girl in my family so I knew from my sisters' experiences that there would be pain involved. All around me people were singing and I couldn't understand why they were so happy – I was terrified. I turned to my sister: 'I really want to run away'.

'Where will you go?' she said.

Her words hit me with a harsh reality. Where could I go? This was my home. My sisters had gone through it; my mother had gone through it and her mother before her. It was a rite of passage and I'd be an outcast in my own family if I didn't go through with it as well. There is no-one to turn to in a situation like that. Even if I had run to the police station, I wouldn't have been helped. The police officers were a part of the community just the same as my family and all the people from the village who were celebrating.

The next morning we were taken out to the bushes where the cutter came. There were four of us: me, my sister, who is two years older than me, and two other girls from the village. I avoided eye-contact with the cutter and only glimpsed her face for a second before closing my eyes. A second was enough for me to never forget how she looked.

In front of us there was an axe inside a bucket of water. It was meant to cool the water they used to clean us, but it didn't help in making it any less painful. My sister was stood to my left. My eyes were closed and I could feel her struggle. She didn't make a single sound. To cry openly would be frowned upon as an embarrassment to the family, but I knew she was crying on the inside. Then it was my turn and I fainted. On coming round I looked down to see I was standing in a pool of my own blood.

It was another 15 years before I could bring myself to speak about what happened that day. Back then, I didn't know to describe it as female genital mutilation. In the Maasai community where I was raised it was a practice deeply rooted in tradition. When something like that happens for so long and no one challenges it, it becomes the normal thing to do, a way of life. FGM happened to me the same as it happened to almost all women in my community.

Female genital mutilation is the term used to describe the partial or total removal of the external female genitalia or other injury to the female genital organs for non-medical reasons. The World Health Organization has classified it into four types depending on the severity of the procedure. I experienced type 1, which involves partial or total removal of the clitoris and/or the prepuce (clitoridectomy). Although this form is the least severe, the memory of the experience haunted me and I felt drawn to challenge the practice and stop it happening to others.

My mother wasn't educated, but she sowed a spark of hope that perhaps I could be. From the age of nine I would walk 15 miles with my mother to fetch water from the river. 'Nashipae,' she would say, 'you don't have to carry all of this if you get an education. You'll build me a big tank and I'll just be going outside of the house to get the water.' So I learned to think that education was the way I could change things. So while many girls in my village got married after going through FGM I told my mother, 'That's not me, that's not what I want for my life. I want an education so that I can help you and my siblings.' I suppose you might say I was different because I wanted my life to be different and I always told myself that no matter what challenges I faced I would pursue an education.

Things are changing now in Kenya, thankfully, but in the 1980s it wasn't considered as important in my community for girls to go to school as it was for boys. It was especially difficult for the youngest girl in a large polygamous family like mine to get an education. In my family I have six half-sisters and three half-brothers, and two older sisters and two younger brothers. My brothers got an education because my father sold cows and a piece of land in order to pay for it. At the time I didn't understand why he couldn't do the same for me, but I was unable to ask him for school fees because in my culture teenage girls were not allowed to speak to their fathers directly about such issues and I always had to speak to my father through my mother. This was sad for me because I'd always had a close relationship with him as a child.

I enjoyed school very much. Unfortunately I kept being thrown out of school because I needed to collect school fees, get a proper uniform, get books and pens, etc. Each morning I'd watch the other children in the village going off to school and it would break my heart later in the day to see them coming back while I made my way home barefoot from the river carrying a jerry can full of water or a heavy load of firewood. At times I felt unbearably sad but the solace I found in church gave me hope. If it wasn't for my faith and belief in God, I would have given up. Every Saturday I would wash the church and decorate it ready for the service on Sunday when I would sing, and for one time in the week I felt alive. Before I left the church, I would always kneel at the altar and pray: 'Please God, don't forget me.' In my heart I believed that God really did have good plans for me, plans that would not only improve my life but would also improve the lives of my family and other women in my village.

Being a curious child, I began to think of ways I could reach out to my father and let him know how I was feeling. Although I wasn't able to talk to him directly, I would often sit with him while he chanted or sang. I wondered if I wrote a poem, if I might be able to him express my feelings to him in that way. So, I wrote a poem in my Maasai mother tongue, and through the verses I pleaded with my father for an education. I wanted him to see that I wasn't different from my brothers in that if I was given the opportunity I could learn and help just like my brothers.

We were sat under a tree when I recited my poem. I called it, 'Take me to school, father.' When I finished reading it I looked up to see my father's reaction – that was the first and last time I saw my father cry. 'I'll make sure you get the best education,' he said. Soon after that he sold one of his favourite bulls to pay for my school fees and then I realised the power of words. A few months later he was diagnosed with cancer and soon after he passed away.

After my father's death I felt an emptiness, a loss of not knowing what to do beyond that. He had given me the hope I was looking for, now I needed to fight for myself. This is when I made a commitment to knock on every possible door irrespective of the 'Nos' I might get along the way.

My father died when I was two years away from graduating from secondary school. I started looking for scholarship opportunities. I approached my secondary school headmistress and poured my heart out to her pleading: 'If you send me back home again, that will be the end of me'. I could see the tears in her eyes when I said that. A few weeks later, she called me to her home and handed me scholarship forms to fill. I was selected for a scholarship and this allowed me to complete my secondary schooling. After that I got a letter from the University. To study for a degree would cost three million Kenyan shillings. I showed my mother the letter and she said: 'Okay we will go to speak to our family members about it'.

Most of my family members didn't consider my request at all because in their view I shouldn't be wasting my time with education, I should be getting married. One family member didn't dismiss the idea immediately, but on hearing what was needed said: 'No-one has three million shillings in their account so we can't afford this and we also have our own families to think about'.

After coming so far in my education the response was disheartening, but my mother helped to keep my hope alive. 'You know what, Nashipae,' she said. 'God will provide the three million in one way or another.' My mother didn't have the money to pay for my fees but we both trusted that we would find the money somehow. Within two years we had the fees and I was in the university.

When I started to talk about coming to the UK people thought I was a joker. I had to face the village elders to justify why I wanted to go. They worried that I wouldn't come back but I told them, 'This is my home, it is where I belong.' I spent six months in York and on coming home I brought some books back with me with the idea of starting a project in my former primary school to help raise the aspirations of young girls. I was amazed at how things had changed in a short time. The same elders who had challenged me about going to the UK were asking if I had any suggestions how to encourage girls to work hard. It was beautiful to see. It felt like I'd proved to them that a girl can achieve the same as a boy.

It felt good to be able to give something back but at the same time I knew those same girls would soon be subjected to FGM and it felt like there was a heavy guilt on my shoulders that I needed to offload.

It took me more than 15 years to stand any conversation about FGM because it brought back such bad memories. I first started to talk about it to close family and friends in Kenya, where, as you can imagine, it is almost normal because so many women have been subjected to FGM. I was aware that people are inclined to continue doing something that has been done by their forefathers and going against that makes them feel they are losing something really important, like they are losing a part of their identity. I knew that I could only bring change if I really pursued an education.

In the UK I met a female doctor who was originally from Uganda. I knew she understood what had happened to me as a child and I felt confident to speak openly with her about FGM. We spent a lot of time talking about the extent of FGM and its impact on girls. Some of the things she was telling me, I had experienced myself or heard other women talk about. I was aware of the complications women can experience, such as the kinds of infections women get, difficulty giving birth, and some women, depending on the severity of the type of FGM they had, find it painful to have sex. However, because all women I knew had gone through FGM we thought that these problems were happening because we were women. Now I knew differently, I started to think, if we used this information well we could change people's perceptions. If the law changes on its own, people will just think that their culture is being attacked, but if we used facts about women's health and how it is impacted then I believed that could really change people's views.

When I talk about ending FGM I try hard not to come across as disrespectful, although I still get accused of that for challenging something that people think is a big part of their cultural identity. One man said to me: 'You shouldn't be calling it mutilation because it's circumcision, just as I am circumcised.'

I said: 'For males it is only the foreskin that is removed; for the female their genitals are mutilated. The only time you can compare FGM to male circumcision is if your penis was to be cut off.'

He went quiet. Sometimes the conversations are really difficult, but if we don't talk, if we don't say how things are, then we won't change anything. My approach is very clear – a sharing of the facts, that FGM is child abuse, it doesn't have any medical benefits, and it's about time we stopped doing it.

Of course, there are some people who are uncomfortable with that, and I can understand why. When a man who comes from a community that practises FGM and his wife has never complained, hears someone like me saying it's a bad thing and he thinks: 'Are you crazy? I'm married to a woman who's been cut and it's never been an issue for her.'

Not talking about FGM is an issue too. For a long time there has been a culture of silence. Thankfully there are now more women speaking about their experiences of FGM and this has given other women the courage to speak out, because the problem is far wider than Africa. Official statistics from the Health and Social Care Information Centre show that 5,484 cases of FGM were recorded in England between October 2014 and September 2015. Although these figures include newly recorded cases of women who were cut many years ago, there is also evidence that FGM is happening in the UK, as well as children being taken away to be cut and then brought back into the country.

There is an argument that FGM is done for men and to please men, but I think that it's time to move beyond the blame game because this is a serious issue for women's health and change has to involve everybody. My mother reminded me of that only recently when she rang to say that my 16-year-old brother would be cut at the end of the year.

'Mother, I know you haven't told me this, but I hope you're not planning to cut the girls,' I said.

'Why?'

'Please don't,' I said.

After that I made continuous calls, trying to convince her not to let my nieces be cut. After listening to my pleas she said: 'You know this is not my decision. It is a decision for the entire community. You need to speak to your brothers and sisters, and your uncles if you feel bold enough.'

'I will do anything for them,' I said. 'Imagine if all the women who have gone through it say my daughter will never be cut – we could break the cycle and end FGM in a generation'.

I spoke to my brother. 'I know this is a really weird topic and I know it's something we don't talk about but I need to tell you'.

He listened then asked me, 'How is she going to fit into society?'

'She will,' I said, 'and if she doesn't, the impact of having it done is far worse than her not fitting into this community. Nothing stops her from living wherever she wants to live.'

I spoke to my aunt too: 'I'm really concerned. I don't want the kids to go through it.'

'Why do you want to spoil it for others?' she said. 'You went through it and name me one single person in our family who has died as a result.'

'There are some complications that we never talk about and they are related to it.' I said.

'Tell me some of them.' I explained to her that I had spoken to a doctor in the UK and what the issues are. 'You think that is because of cutting?' she asked me.

'I do.'

Last year we made a collective decision as a family that for us, FGM ended with me. We broke the culture of silence. No women in our family will have to go through FGM again, and my family are now advocates for change, campaigning against it.

11 How we respond

Emily Finch

Emily Finch grew up in the North Yorkshire coastal town of Filey and after training in youth work felt called to explore different ways to help churches reach out to their surrounding communities. Together with some like-minded people, she created The Bus Stop in 2015, a charity which helps churches to build relationships with young people, communities and schools.

> **'For it was you who formed my inward parts; you knit me together in my mother's womb I praise you, for I am fearfully and wonderfully made. Wonderful are your works; that I know very well' (Ps. 139:13-14).**

John Sentamu writes:

We have often heard the cliché, 'If you want to be able to love others, you have to learn to love yourself.' But like many clichés it has a core of truth. In a society where young people's poor self-image can often result in self-harm, or harm of others, we are very aware of the need to help them find a new way of understanding themselves. A way of knowing they are worthy of love, and so able to love others.

Emily's story shows how a bold step of imagination, faith and generosity have given her the opportunity to reach out to young people where they are – and help them towards an understanding of God's great love for them. God created us all *'in his own image and likeness'* (Genesis 1:26-27). And, as Psalm 139 says, that means that we are all *'Fearfully and wonderfully made'*. That doesn't mean we all look – or act – like sanitised saints. No matter what, God loves us as his adopted children in Christ Jesus. When we know we are loved, it makes us feel 10 feet tall and capable of anything. How great that God's love can make us feel like that every day. Do not aspire to be like angels. For he *'made us a little lower than the angels, and crowned us with glory and honour'* (Psalm 8:5).

✝

If you've grown up going to Sunday services it can be hard to imagine how difficult it is for some people to step inside a church. There are people in churches who want to get involved in their community and to build relationships beyond the church walls. Wouldn't it be fantastic if there was a way to make it easier to get together? The Bus Stop is my way of helping to bridge that gap.

I'd been toying with the idea of a mobile centre for Christian youth work for a while. I knew that a church in York, St Michael le Belfrey, owned an old double-decker bus it rarely used. The thought of using it as a community centre was amazing – a large space that could be moved to wherever needed it most. I imagined it rocking up to my home town of Filey on the North Yorkshire coast when I was a teenager. When I was growing up it felt like nothing exciting ever happened in Filey – perhaps this could be a way to make church fun, and rural life as well.

I let the idea run away with me but although I had the enthusiasm for it, I couldn't see practically how to make it work. I knew little about cars and even less about buses. I had no idea how much a bus would cost or what the upkeep would involve. Thinking that perhaps my dream was unrealistic, I tried to let it go, in so far as I wasn't consciously thinking about it. As much as I tried to ignore it, the idea didn't leave me alone. Something inside was telling me to just go for it and buy the bus. The only way to describe it is: if I were to say, God isn't calling me to buy a bus, I knew it would be a lie.

It felt bold and cheeky to go to St Michael le Belfrey church and ask their youth worker, Lee, if I could buy their bus. I did it anyway.

When I asked, Lee said: 'How did you know it was for sale?' It wasn't the response I'd been expecting. All I could think to say in response was, 'Wow!' I hadn't known the bus was for sale, only that it wasn't being used. Suddenly my dream was real or at least within my grasp and it hit me with a rush of both excitement and fear. What to do next?

I prayed and talked it over with some good friends whose opinions I value. My overarching feeling was that I should use my savings to buy it. A lot of people thought the idea was bonkers, but for me it felt like another stage in learning to trust God with my life. It felt like a bold step, but if I believed that if I could trust God with anything, then that had to include my finances as well. The tricky bit would be to convince my parents; after all it was their savings I would be spending.

I wanted to buy the bus using money my parents had put aside for me over the years. I rang them and said: 'I'm just going to put this idea out there. We won't chat about it now, I just thought I'd let it simmer.' There was silence on the other end so I continued, 'You know how every time I follow God it works? Every time I think God is saying something it always turns out to be the best thing ever…'

'Oh no, what is it?' my dad said.

'Well, I think God is calling me to buy a double-decker bus to use in youth work.'

'Great, that sounds fun,' my mum said.

'And I think that I should use the savings that you've put aside for me to buy it,' I added quickly.

'What!'

I knew that it was an idea that might take some getting used to so I quickly ended the call. 'That's it. That's what I had to tell you, bye.' I hung up and let them simmer for a while.

Later we chatted about it at length and my dad said: 'If that's what you feel you should use the money for then that's fine with us.' I could feel my smile through my whole body. It felt good to have that trust and support from my parents. So I did it. I went back to see Lee and I bought his double-decker bus.

The bus was kept in an old barn along with a load of other old buses. It was a kind of playground for bus enthusiasts, which worked out to be another blessing. I've kept the bus there and if anything goes wrong, there is always someone on hand who is willing and able to fix it. One of the men I met there goes to a church which now uses the bus. He offered to give me driving lessons for free. It was like all the problems I'd worried about initially were being removed one by one – it was amazing.

A couple I'd never met heard about what I was doing and donated money for the bus to be refurbished and painted. Friends who were good at DIY came to help me, and I learned how to use a screwdriver so I could do my bit too. The result is not your usual double-decker bus. It's a vibrant purple with welcoming signs letting people know that it is a space for young people and communities. The riding seats have been taken out to create a social space. Upstairs there is a kitchen, comfy seating and a TV on the back wall. The downstairs is often used as a community café and has sofas, coffee machines and a massive craft table for the kids.

Initially I thought I should get a part-time job and do some paid work alongside the project. I did that for a while but it was difficult to juggle both and I felt as if God was saying to me, 'I've given you this mission and you need to do it wholeheartedly.' In other words, I felt that the bus should be my full-time focus. I stopped doing the part-time job and since then I have never had to worry about money. I'm not loaded by any means, but God has provided every step of the way in incredible ways.

Our first booking came from Church Army officers on the Flaxley Road estate in Selby. The building they'd been using on the estate wasn't available any more so they were looking for a new space. When they booked the bus, I was still taking bus driving lessons and wasn't fully ready. I was grateful for the trust they placed in me and that they shared the vision I had for what the bus could be. Now every Wednesday we park outside the local primary school in the centre of the estate. Two Church Army officers from the estate are on board with me, because the idea is not that I sweep in as a novelty, but that the space is used by the local church enabling more people in the community get to know them. During the day we hold a community café and straight after school we get lots of mums coming on board with their children, who love the sweet shop upstairs. In the evening our focus changes to young people and we move the bus into the school car park where we have a youth drop-in and youth Alpha group.

Our work now is a mix of regular stops and one-off missions. Often people will come on board and ask what it's all about. We tell them that the local church is here to get to know people in the community. Sometimes that will spark a conversation and other times that will be all a person wants to know. Some people who come along aren't interested in God or exploring faith but they still want to join us because they love the atmosphere on board and that's fine. For us, the bus is about getting to know people and loving them for who they are and where they are at right now. Some people are adamant they don't want to talk about God when they first step on the bus, but when they get to know us often these same people start asking questions about God and faith. It comes up in a natural way if people are curious to know more, there is no need to force it.

The Gospel is contagious and we can't hide that. We're always open about why we do what we do. For example, we have a prayer post box inside. Next to it are some paper and pens for people to write down whatever is on their mind and post it. Whatever is on those notes, we pray about that week. During drop-in groups we always have fifteen minutes of prayer at the end of the evening. It's clear what we're doing because I'll say, 'If you want to stay you can join in with the prayer. If you don't want to, that's the end of the night.' A lot of the young people aren't interested in staying for that final part of the evening but for some experiencing prayer has been about them connecting with God in a new way. In this sense it's not about the words we say when we pray together, rather it's about these young people experiencing God themselves.

Recently, we had so many young people sign up to a service that we were unsure if we'd have space for them all. At first I wondered if they knew it was youth worship they were coming along to, but when I asked they said they did and yet still more wanted to come along. I was overjoyed at the response but once we started I could feel irritation growing inside me as one boy sniggered all the way through the service. He laughed at my prayers, he laughed at what other people had to say, everything about it was a joke to him. I was annoyed because I'd been clear at the outset what the event was. This was supposed to be a time we could spend together with God and he wasn't taking any of it seriously.

We had set up some prayer stations for private reflection after the service. The same boy who had sniggered all the way through later came up to me and said: 'I can't read these prayer stations.' Trying to hide my irritation I took a deep breath and said: 'All right. I'll walk round with you and tell you what they say. Is that ok?'

'Yep, that's fine,' he said, but to me it didn't sound like he wanted to do it.

The first prayer station was a simple activity where we asked people to identify their good qualities and in doing so recognise that we are unique and that everyone has different strengths. The boy's task was to write down all the things that were good about him and then thank God for those things. 'What's good about you?' I asked.

'Nothing,' he said.

'What?' I felt that this boy was testing my patience too far and very soon it was about to show.

'There's nothing good about me,' he said. 'I can't think of one thing. There's nothing.'

I could tell by his eyes that he believed this to be true and suddenly I saw him in a completely different light. Here was the class clown, the loud-mouth who moments earlier was difficult and uninterested, telling me that he couldn't think of a single good thing about himself. My heart went out to him. I wished he could sense even the tiniest part of his worth to God. I wanted to tell him: don't you know how precious you are to God? I didn't say this, because it wouldn't mean anything to the boy. Instead I had to figure out from talking to him what he was probably good at, to find at least one thing to change his view that there was nothing good about him. We did get something down on paper and looking at it he asked, 'So what do I do with this, now?'

'You take it home and you stick it on your wall somewhere you can see it,' I said. 'Every day when you look at it, remind yourself what's good about you. Thank God for those things and whenever you think of some more things that are good about you add those to the list as well.'

I've since met lots of teenagers who can't think of anything good about themselves. It still shocks me every time I hear them say it. Now, instead of asking teenagers to think of something good about themselves I'll often ask them to say something good about the person sitting next to them. Sometimes, even when they hear it from a friend, they find it hard to believe those good things about themselves. I also share Bible verses with them, about how they are 'wonderfully made'. I tell them that this is not something that I've made up, it's what God says to each one of us, and it is up to us as individuals how we respond to that.

For my part, following God has been an adventure and I'm taking each step as it comes. I didn't know what to expect when I set up The Bus Stop, but I feel that I couldn't have picked a better job for myself. I think God knows better than we do what is good for us. I know that in my heart, but as much as we can tell people that God is great and God is good our words can't express what it feels like to know that deep inside. My hope for The Bus Stop is that through our work we help people to experience God and all his wonder for themselves.

12 Going into the unknown

John Senior

Major John Senior MBE TD is Lifeboat Operations Manager at Scarborough Lifeboat Station, a volunteer role that is offered by invitation of the lifeboat Coxswain and the crew. On 22 February 2015, Humber Coastguard made an emergency call to the town's lifeboat station – Andrew McGeown, a man known personally to John and many of the crew, was in difficulties in the sea.

'No one has greater love than this, to lay down one's life for one's friends' (John 15:13).

John Sentamu writes:

On a sunny day in May 2012, I sailed, at the helm, into Whitby on the RNLI lifeboat 'George and Mary Webb'. The passage was smooth when I made that trip, but I know that the work of that and other lifeboats on our dangerous coastline has brought hope and life to many desperate people as they struggle in mountainous seas and terrible weather.

Major John Senior's story shows the terrifying and perilous task that our lifeboat men and women face every time they go out on a rescue mission. But though they know the real risks they face, their courage, discipline and determination carry them through. Losing their friend whom they had battled so hard to save was a deep grief for them, but it will not discourage them from taking those same risks again.

When Jesus Christ came to earth from heaven, he was setting out on a dangerous mission to rescue us – similar to Saving Private Ryan - a mission which cost him his own life. But in doing so, he rescued all of us, plucking us out of the deep waters of Sin, the Flesh, the World and the Devil, and bringing us safe to shore. Jesus Christ is ever ready to reach out that saving hand to us, if we will let him grasp us and bring us into his warm embrace. He is the Good Shepherd who *'leaves the ninety-nine on the mountain and goes in search of the one that went astray and brings it home rejoicing'* (Matthew 18:12-13; Luke 15:4-7).

✝

I'd not long sat down to Sunday dinner when the call came through. It was about 6pm, and by this time in February the sun had already gone down. We had information that someone was in the water, so it was a full shout, which means all available lifeboat crews respond and race for the station.

As Lifeboat Operations Manager, I am responsible for releasing the crew to launch the boat. Before launching the lifeboat we take into account everything that is going on at that moment – the type and location of the incident, the number of casualties involved and most importantly what the prevailing weather and sea conditions are likely to be – and then we make the decision to go to sea or not. My responsibility is to make sure that the crews go to sea safely and come back safely, but if they choose not to go, it's not like the army, I have no authority to make them go. Each member of the team has to decide to respond to the bleeper; to put down their knife and fork, switch off the TV, get out of bed, leave the house, whatever it is they are doing at that moment, and respond to the call. They are all volunteers and once that 'yellow line' goes there are few resources left to back them up. There is the Coast Guard Search and Rescue helicopter, but if conditions are poor the helicopter won't be able to get in to help. The crew go into the unknown and once that lifeboat is out to sea these guys are pretty much on their own.

I've never known a crew refuse to launch. Often the jobs are routine and not particularly dangerous, but once in a while there is a call asking the crew to go into extremely difficult circumstances where their lives could be at risk. You might call it foolhardy to launch at the dead of night into the teeth of a raging gale, particularly when the information is sketchy and there is no guarantee of a positive outcome. Basically, even in the best conditions there is only about 20 minutes between someone getting into trouble in the water and drowning. In the winter, survival times can be as low as four minutes, yet even knowing this, to do nothing would be harder for the crew to deal with because of the ethos of duty and self-sacrifice ingrained in the RNLI mentality.

There is a sense of comradeship between crew members and a deep awareness of the great traditions of the Lifeboat service. We are continually inspired by the actions of the heroes of years gone by and the lengths to which they went to in order to save lives at sea, often facing the most horrendous of conditions with only very basic of equipment. In situations like that you rely on your faith to see you through, because there is little else to hang on to.

On the night of 22 February 2015 when we took the call, we knew the man in the water; he was Andrew McGeown, a 32-year-old roofer who was friends with soldiers I'd served with in the army and an old school pal of a couple of the lifeboat crew. That night he was walking his dog with a friend around the Spa approach in Scarborough. The wind and rain made it a miserable night for a walk but that area is usually very safe. There were no other dogs around, so Andrew let his dog off the lead. The Staffordshire bull terrier jumped up onto the sea wall, but as he did there was a swell coming in and a wave covered them, lifting the dog into the sea. Andrew, who was wearing wet-weather builder's gear, jumped over the sea wall to save his pet. I don't think he realised that the tide had come in as far as it had. What he'd thought was waist deep water was six-feet of swirling sea water. Being a strong, robust guy, Andrew managed to catch his dog and lift him to safety. He then grabbed his friend's hand in the hope it would give him the lift needed to pull him back over the sea wall, but as he tried to climb back up the wall a wave knocked him off his feet. Managing to find his footing again he made a clamp out of his hands and his friend's. They held on for as long as they could, but it was clear they were now in a lot of trouble. His friend started shouting for help, but he could hold on no longer. The swell brought a high wave crashing down and the force of it broke their grip and swept Andrew further out to sea.

We deployed the ILB, which is the bright orange, inshore rubber lifeboat. There was a crew of three: helmsman, Rudi Barman, aged 36 and crewmen, Craig Burnett, aged 45 and Adam Beston, aged 30. When they left their homes on what they thought would be a routine call, it turned out to be something very different. The launch was inside the conditions allowed for that lifeboat to deploy, but once on the scene the storm was worse than anticipated. Going to sea in a five metre long boat in a force gale is terrifying. It's like being put into a washing machine. There was a big swell and the wind was driving waves in from all directions. The crew could have backed-off and nobody would have thought the worse of them, but they carried on nonetheless.

On-shore the coastguard's search lights were shining into the water, but the combination of the darkness and heavy seas meant that for most of the time, Andrew was lost from view. As the lights panned across the water the crew spotted

Andrew, face down in the water, against the sea wall, but they couldn't get the boat into a position to be close enough to reach him. Waves crashed over the sea wall while others rebounded from it, causing confused and dangerous conditions. The crew had their eyes on Andrew, but as they tried to get closer he disappeared from view again. Calculating that the tide would sweep Andrew southwards on an eddy, Rudi reversed towards the shore several times, ready to power away should a large wave threaten them. On one approach the engine lost power and the boat almost capsized. Rudi managed to get it going again and because they thought they saw an arm go up and over, the crew kept going back into the surf.

Having lost sight of Andrew, the crew started a series of searches parallel to the beach. The rescue helicopter arrived and with its lights shining on the water Adam spotted a reflection that he believed to be Andrew some twenty metres from the shore. Keeping him in sight Rudi sped the boat to within reaching distance. They managed to grab Andrew but the conditions were such that it was unsafe to stop the boat in the heavy surf so close to the shore. While the crew kept tight hold of Andrew, Rudi steered the boat to calmer seas where they were able to get him on-board. Craig, a fully-trained paramedic, immediately began cardiopulmonary resuscitation (CPR) as the lifeboat sped back to the harbour. On shore life-saving efforts of the RNLI continued with volunteers, Dr Peter Billingsley, Head of Clinical Services for Scarborough Hospital and Jason Hedges, another paramedic, taking over. The whole crew took it in turns to administer CPR continuously for about twenty minutes until the ambulance arrived. If there was any chance of recovery, the team gave it to Andrew, but sadly fifteen minutes after arriving at Scarborough hospital he was pronounced dead. In truth, Andrew was drowned before they got to him, but the team went through their life-saving cycle all the same, never giving up until what they had feared was confirmed.

It is always shocking to lose a life, but for the crew to recover the body of a friend was particularly difficult. After a rescue like this, the boat, full of body fluids, has to be taken apart and fully cleaned. Yet, within ten minutes of reaching the shore the lifeboat station was back to operations, and if another call came in, it perhaps could have been that same crew who would've responded.

I know that the crew don't remember the day for skilled boatmanship and bravery in high seas. They remember it as the day a young man and a friend lost his life at sea, and their devastation at not being able to save him. All who witnessed the rescue, however, recognised the courage, skill and dedication it took to bring Andrew back to shore.

In recognition of his leadership and boat handling that night, Rudi, the helmsman, was awarded a RNLI Bronze Medal for Gallantry – the first RNLI Gallantry Medal to be awarded to a Scarborough RNLI volunteer since 1973. For their team work, courage and perseverance, Craig Burnett and Adam Beston both received RNLI framed letters of thanks signed by the Chairman; and Dr Peter Billingsley and Jason Hedges received Operations Director's letters of thanks.

It was a tragic outcome, but Andrew's family recognised too that the RNLI volunteers risked everything in their efforts to save their friend. Since Andrew McGeown's death, his family and friends have begun working with the RNLI to create a legacy fund in his memory. In the first year they raised more than £11,000 which is being used to ensure that safety messages reach local people and visitors to the Yorkshire coast, as well as paying for swimming safety lessons for children and young people in the area.

Right now there are five people sitting in Scarborough with their bleepers on who won't be going more than two or three miles away from the town centre, and that role is mirrored in the 280 lifeboat stations across the country. These volunteers are on call and after their shift they will hand over to another team and that goes on 24 hours a day, seven days a week. No matter what they are doing when a call comes in, those men and women respond, and they never know when that might be because the bleeper always goes off at the most unexpected times.

13 An incredible journey

Kate Marsden

Kate Marsden and her husband John spent thirteen years working for international relief and development organisation, Food for the Hungry, in Bangladesh, where she introduced a programme to help people to live out the gospel in a practical way that enhanced their lives and the lives of those around them. Together they now run Mustard Seeds Shared, an overseas aid charity that shares small but powerful ideas which when applied faithfully produce big and lasting results.

'Trust in the Lord with all your heart, and do not rely on your own insight. In all your ways acknowledge him, and he will make straight your paths.'
(Proverbs 3:5-6)

John Sentamu writes:

In Uganda we have many proverbs which we use day by day: 'It takes a whole village to raise a child'; 'The person who never travels thinks their mother is the best cook'. 'A stick in your neighbour's home can't chase a menacing leopard at your door.' Little sayings which contain something profound about the way we live our lives.

The Book of Proverbs is full of wise observations and advice, which prove true in every generation and in every culture. These two verses from Proverbs 3: 5-6 contain three pieces of advice and a promise.

The Advice - 1. Trust in the Lord with all your heart; 2. Don't just rely on what you think you know; 3. Acknowledge that God acts in everything you do. And the Promise: He will make your way clear.

Kate's story shows that just relying on her own ideas and inclinations didn't really work. She felt anxious and uncertain when it seemed that her life was not going in the direction she wanted. But when she accepted that God was calling her to follow a particular path, then she began to see how he was also making that path easier to follow. May we find that this Proverb is true for all our lives.

Let us recognise our need. Go to the one who can meet that need – Jesus Christ. And let us live the way of Jesus Christ. For he is *'the Way, the Truth and the Life'* (John 14:6).

✟

When people find out my husband and I are missionaries they often ask: 'How many people have become Christians through your work?'

At one time I too might have thought that was our role. Now, I say: 'Please ask us another question. Ask us how we see God working in people's lives.'

This year I celebrated my 65th birthday. It was a big occasion, not simply because I'd reached a new milestone, but because in the same month we had cause for a triple celebration – my husband, John's 60th birthday and our ruby wedding anniversary. So much has happened in those past 40 years, and it is only by looking back that we can see how each stage of our lives was preparing us for what was to come. Of course, God in his wisdom never frightens us with what is further down the road. If he had, we might never have had the courage to step on the path and would have missed out on an incredible journey.

I met John at Glasgow University and we got married while we were students. Our commitment must have seemed to some as outrageously youthful. 25 years later we didn't have the naivety of youth on our side. So why did we leave behind everything we'd known – our home, family, friends, and jobs – to go and live in Bangladesh? How could we do that? The short answer is, 'We couldn't.' It was one of those occasions where if we'd known where we would end up before we set off, we never would have made the journey. It would have felt impossible – as if we were being asked to give up everything that was important to us. It was a step-by-step process and God, in his graciousness, took us one step at a time.

The first of those steps was taken long before I met John. As a child, from about the age of five, I wanted to be a missionary. My family were members of a Baptist church and sometimes visiting missionaries to the parish would stay with us. I enjoyed hearing their stories and saving coins in a little box, so we could give something towards helping children living in the far-off countries where the missionaries worked. When I was 11 years old, I was given a biography of William Carey, who founded the English Baptist Missionary Society and lived in India for 41 years. I remember the missionary who gave it to me saying to my mother, 'God has got something very special for this child.' His words only strengthened what I already dreamed of – I wanted to be a missionary. I later heard that to do mission work I needed to be a doctor or a nurse, so I did all I could to study medicine.

By the time I met John I'd already had a taste of working overseas, having spent some time as a student doctor in a mission hospital in Uganda. While I was enjoying my first experience of living outside of the UK, John was getting used to being back on home soil. His father was a Presbyterian minister and the family moved to Singapore when John was in his early teens. Today we think of Singapore as a wealthy, vibrant, clean, and beautiful city state. Back then it was quite different. You could walk into the market place and it was all hustle and bustle with people shouting for you to buy their produce. There was a shanty house over the fence from the manse where John's family lived. It wasn't the same poverty I'd witnessed in Africa, but it was clear that people were struggling and everyone was working hard so life could be better.

I later learned how John too had been influenced early on by visiting speakers at his church. He remembers being given a book as a child. It was Chinese and when he opened it, John was fascinated to discover that you started at the back and went forwards, reading up and down instead of left to right. 'It was intriguing as a young child,' he said, 'It made me realise that there were other parts of the world, places that were different.'

We both saw ourselves leaving university and living abroad, but when we graduated we couldn't get the work we'd hoped for. In hindsight, we were applying for jobs that we weren't fully qualified for – we had the academic skills, but not the life experience. Instead, we found ourselves moving to York, where John got a place to study a Masters in health economics. During that time we both found work locally with the NHS, John as a manager and later I got a job as a community health doctor. It wasn't long before we became parents for the first time, when our daughter, Ruth, was born and shortly after our son, David, followed. All our energies were taken up with work and family, and feeling settled in the community we made York our home.

It was many years later before the idea of doing any kind of missionary work came up again. Through our church, St Michael le Belfrey, we met the UK representatives of an international Christian relief development organisation called Food for the Hungry. Through that friendship I found myself going to help set up a programme for refugees in Uvira, in the Democratic Republic of Congo. It was wonderful to be back in Africa again. All the things I'd loved about my first visit to the continent were still there: the vibrant colours, the music, and the openness of the people. When I came home John and I thought that it would be lovely if we could do some similar work as a family. Our children were now 16 and 17 years old, and we thought perhaps it was about time that they learned there was more to the world than the comfortable bits. The only volunteer opportunities available at that time were in Bangladesh, so that's where we went.

I loved the people we met that summer and I enjoyed being able to help out in a school, but I didn't share my family's enthusiasm to do it all again. When John, Ruth and David were saying, 'Thank you for a lovely holiday, we'd love to see you again', I said a relieved: 'Goodbye!' I was absolutely shattered and couldn't wait to get back in my own bed for a good night's sleep.

When we returned home it was clear that my family had fallen head over heels for Bangladesh. Before going to university both our children chose to take a gap year volunteering in Dhaka, and John became increasingly involved with volunteer projects, resigning from his job to set up as a freelance consultant so as to be able to spend more time working for Food for the Hungry.

Three years after our first summer in Bangladesh four country director positions became available at the charity – three in Africa and one in Bangladesh. My heart longed to go back to Africa, but for various reasons those positions became unavailable leaving Bangladesh as the only option.

I wasn't sure that I would be able to go. Since our first trip John had travelled back to Bangladesh a couple of times, but I didn't join him. After spending a month in Dhaka, I did question whether I could cope with life there. The climate was so hot and humid there wasn't a night I slept through.

It wasn't just the lack of sleep that got me down during that first visit; I was also starting to feel oppressed as a woman. I'd been told that while in Bangladesh I must never look into the eye of a man, because that would be giving the wrong impression. The message was given to me in such a strong manner that I never looked above my shoes. I'd lived like that for a month, but how would I cope if that was my every day? More than that, how could I leave my life in York and everything I knew?

At the time David was just about to go to university. Both he and Ruth were excited at the idea of mum and dad having a place to visit in Bangladesh, but I had always assumed we would have a home base for them in York, at least until they got married or had homes of their own. At the same time as the job came up my dad was very ill. He needed a lot of care and I was helping to look after him. How could I go and live half-way across the world, when there was so much for me to do at home?

I started talking all these things over with God. One day in my prayers I said: 'God, you promised me you'd look after my dad.' Soon after that I began to feel calmness about the situation. It was like I'd had an insight, that everything would be ok – as if God was saying to me, 'I will look after your dad, but I didn't say that you would look after him.'

People would say to me, 'How can you leave your dad?' I couldn't answer because I didn't know. Others would say to me: 'How can you go when David is just going to university? This is the time when people should be home for their kids' and again I'd reply, 'I don't know how we can go, I just know that we are going.'

We made the decision to go to Bangladesh in October 1998 and flew to Dhaka the following summer. My dad died three months before we left and I was able to be with him close to the end, something I am so grateful for. I still don't know if I could have left knowing he was so ill. It was one of those times when I found myself saying yes to something without knowing how or even if I was able to do it.

John's assignment as a country director was initially for two years. Thankfully our apartment had air conditioning, which made it easier to sleep. When the power cuts came, which was often, I'd wake up drenched in sweat. It was then I realised that the Bangladeshi people don't sleep in the heat either. I could hear them talking and singing – they were as uncomfortable as we were, they just didn't complain. I told myself - if they could get up the next day and work, so could I.

The problem was: I didn't have a job to do. Every day I would go into the office and ask if anyone needed any help with anything. If they did, I'd do it, but officially I was the accompanying spouse, which meant that there was no role for me. As a woman in Bangladesh it was like I was invisible – sometimes I didn't even feel like a person, but I felt like God was saying to me, 'You're my daughter; you don't need to bow your head.' I made my way along the same streets I'd walked many times before, but this time I kept my head up and lowered my eyes. Many people wouldn't even have noticed I was doing anything differently, but this one action had a huge impact on how I felt about myself. It no longer mattered as much that I couldn't go out of the apartment on my own or that I had to wear a sari. I thought: if I can hold my head up high, I can live here. Lots of people told me, 'If you don't have a role you won't survive'. What kept me going was my firm belief that if God has called one member of a couple then he has called them both, so I'd tell them in reply: 'God hasn't yet shown me my role.'

In comparison, John had a very clear purpose. He had an organisation to run, staff to manage and if they were doing a really good job then we were going to have much more of an impact on poverty than anything we could do by handing notes out of a car window in Dhaka. Here poverty was in our faces and we could give every penny we had and spend all our time handing out money to people who were begging and we'd not make any significant impact on it at all. Yes, we might help a few people, but if we stood on a street corner and started handing out money we'd be overwhelmed by the crowd of poverty very quickly. We had to come to terms with the fact that we couldn't solve it all and we needed to focus on the work the organisation was doing, which is about sustainable long-term solutions.

In some ways the poverty you see on the city's streets is not the worst of it. There are other people who can't even make it to that point – women back in the village, who've probably never held the equivalent of more than £1 in the palm of their hand their whole lives; women whose husbands pedal rickshaws and only eat when he gets good fares and if he doesn't, they struggle.

Many families in the villages had lost their land because the river banks had been eroded and the land washed away. They were struggling in shanties, trying to rebuild their lives. When we first met women in this situation and asked what their hopes were for the future they had no answer. They were poor and believed there was nothing they could do to improve their situation. Food for the Hungry came along and asked these same women to join a savings group of about 15 women. Through the scheme they began to save tiny amounts every week until they had built up enough money as a group to do something with it. Instead of buying rice by the bag each day or week, depending on when they had enough money, they were able to buy a sack of rice at harvest time. It sounds like a small thing, but one woman told me, 'For the first time in our lives our families have not been hungry'.

When we went back to the same group two years later they couldn't stop talking about what they'd done, how much their lives had changed and what their hopes were for the future. Hope had burst in them and out of that hope grew a confidence that they could change their situation. To be a part of an organisation that was helping people to make those kinds of changes was hugely satisfying.

It was important to us that the people we worked with were developing spiritually as well as economically. In many ways, that was the bigger challenge. John asked me if I could develop some staff training on the values and vision of the organisation. This became my role and I'm glad it unfolded in this way because had I known it earlier, I wouldn't have thought it was something I could do. Later I would go on to develop simple biblical values lessons for the poor women our staff served.

I'm not a teacher and I've never been to Bible school, so in many ways I was learning too. I began to ask myself: what does it mean for me to be a Christian? If I am a follower of Jesus, how does that impact on how I live my life?

The staff would read the bible together as a group, especially the books of Moses, the Psalms and the Gospels. Many were hearing these words for the first time, and their questions began to raise new questions in me. These were stories I had heard so many times yet their words began to resonate in my life in a new way as I began to see people change their behaviour because of the stories they had read. My faith became bigger in a sense because I saw so many different ways in which God brings us close to him, and how a practical faith has the power to spread his love through a community in ways I could never have imagined.

That is why I don't see our role as missionaries to bring people to identify themselves as Christians. Instead, ask us how we see God working in people's lives and we will tell you stories of forgiveness and reconciliation within families and communities; of fathers becoming fathers – showing patience rather than beating their children, listening to them, teaching their daughters to ride bicycles when other men only teach their sons; stories not simply of one person in our office changing his behaviour, but of whole families and communities changing. That change comes from God and it's been such a privilege for us to be part of it.

14   *Together we can*

Gabriel Oyediwura

Gabriel Oyediwura is a youth worker for the M13 Youth Project in Ardwick, Manchester, which works with more than 500 young people every year to encourage action and positive change. After experiencing what it's like to be wrongly labelled by association, Gabriel has focused his work on helping to get young people's voices heard, enabling them to recognise their ability to change their communities for the better.

'For just as the body is one and has many members, and all the members of the body, though many, are one body, so it is with Christ' (1 Corinthians 12:12).

John Sentamu writes:

The Apostle Paul in his First Letter to the Corinthians gives this wonderful image of all followers of Jesus Christ as members of one body. When all the parts of a body are working well together, it can do marvellous things – run a marathon, discover penicillin, write a symphony, together send a person to the moon. But when it isn't working in harmony it stumbles, or falls sick, and is a problem for those around it.

Gabriel's story tells of the ways in which being part of a body can be a blessing or a problem. Many young people join a gang because they want to belong, to be accepted – to be part of something greater than themselves. But that kind of body can often be at war with itself – and with others.

As Gabriel was growing up he saw dangers that even a loose association with gangs created. The threat and reality of violence was a destructive force in the wider body of the community. Happily, he found other groups which became a blessing and a real practical and loving support in his life. And just as he was sustained and helped to grow, so now, he works to help other young people see the power for good of a caring involvement in society. As the African proverb says, 'When a tiny toe is hurting, the whole body stoops down to attend to that toe.' As the Body of Christ let us together bend all our energies to attend to all who are hurting in his body and in his world.

✠

I have never been in a gang, but when you move in similar circles as gang members, like I did, it is easy to get stigmatised. At the time I was a teenager, I was just hanging out. I can't say that I ever had any intention or motive to be in a gang, but by association I got labelled. I remember the first time I was stopped and searched by the police. I was 17 years old and was walking down an alley with a group of friends at about 4 o'clock in the afternoon. We were told that we were being searched because we were a large group of males. I emptied my pockets and I was carrying two phones. I said: 'One is for business and one is for pleasure' – wrong answer. It didn't do to play smart. One police officer made a comment about drug dealers carrying two phones. I was pushed against the wall and searched. I had nothing on me and so the police had to let me go. Looking back I can see from the police's point of view we were all guys in hoods and they assumed living where we were, we were all gang members. I'm 6ft 2 and weigh 16 stone, but I never saw myself as the threat some other people saw me as. Seeing myself in this way, even though it was wrong, shook me up and as big as I am, I walked away from that situation crying and angry.

It was shortly after that one of my friends was shot and killed. He had family members who were involved with gang members, but as far as I was aware he was never involved in gang activity himself. It's likely the shooting was a case of mistaken identity. He was 16 years old and his death dealt a hard blow to many people living on the estate. My mum was fearful. We'd moved to Manchester from London when I was a small child to escape gang culture on our estate. Now we were surrounded by it again, but this time I was older and had my own views and opinions on what I wanted to do, who I wanted to hang out with, what was safe and what wasn't.

My mum didn't want me to go to my friend's funeral. She said it was because the funeral was being held in a community where another gang killing had taken place and there had been a reprisal during the wake. What if there was a revenge attack at this funeral in the same way? 'My friend wasn't in a gang,' I said.

'No, but he was killed at the hands of gang members and there are members of his family there who know who did it and why,' my mum replied.

I didn't listen. Going to the funeral was something I felt I had to do, so I did. When something like that happens in your life you can't ignore it, it changes you. For me, I remember standing looking at his coffin thinking, what is life? The answer that came back to me was: life is precious.

What happened for me after that was a combination of many moments that reinforced this belief that life is precious and I wanted to do everything I could to make my life better for me and for other people. I've since realised that I was surrounded by a lot of love and prayers at that time. My mum and my sister would always pray for me when I went out on the streets, because sometimes things happen and you don't need to have done anything to be the one who gets the raw end.

During this time I started going to a youth club run by M13 Youth Project, where I'd play cards and sit and chat. Sometimes we'd talk about serious stuff like relationships and gangs and faith, but what kept me going back was the banter, the jokes and the closeness of having people around who gave me their time and really listened. Once I got to know them, I felt I could express anything and it was safe. After I'd been going to the youth club for a couple of years one of the leaders, Helen, asked me if I'd like to speak at the theological college where she works about what it feels like to be associated with gang culture when you have never committed a crime yourself. I agreed to do the talk, and being at the college opened my eyes to the idea of me being a Christian youth worker. Before that I hadn't known there was a college where you could learn to do that kind of work. The realisation, along with a decision I'd made at my mum's church to give my life to Christ, and a desire to give back something to the community in the same way M13 had supported me, all led me to where I am today. I texted Helen to say, I think I'd like to become a youth worker, and she helped me from there.

M13 supported me through every step, from my studies to a work placement and into my first job. The majority of our work is detached youth work, which means that I spend most of my time out on the streets, meeting new people and building relationships. Luckily for me the project is well established in our area, so there is an element of trust already there. Through my conversations with young people I can help to direct them to projects and services based on their interests and needs. For me, the best part of my job is when a young person comes to me with an issue and I'm able to give them time to reflect on it by being there and listening from a place of love. Seeing them come to a decision that takes them to a better place and being able to walk alongside them at those important moments fills me with joy.

There are times when I get disheartened because someone doesn't want to accept my help. In those times I tell myself to keep an open heart so that the lines of communication can stay open in case that person wants to come back for support another time. To hold any kind of resentment wouldn't enable that to happen, because people can sense it. I know first-hand what it's like for people to assume bad things about me that aren't true and it isn't nice. Thankfully, times have changed since I was young. There is more awareness of stop and search, and the police aren't as volatile as they once were. That doesn't mean there aren't other social issues that affect young people's lives, of course there are, and I've found that young people still feel just as disempowered and frustrated as I did at that age.

When faced with a societal issue it can feel like we're one person against the system. What can we do? Running up to the 2015 general election I began to realise most of the young adults around me felt disconnected from what was happening. They had a vote the same as everyone else and yet when I spoke to them it was clear that most of them believed that their vote didn't count. They told me that they weren't going to vote; they had never voted in the past and couldn't see themselves voting in the future because it was a waste of time.

I've voted at elections, but when I heard the viewpoints of the young adults around me I started to think about why I voted. I suppose at first I wasn't consciously aware of what was going on politically. I simply voted Labour because that is what my mum did and she had brought me up to understand that my vote was important. I realised that telling these young adults how previous generations had struggled to win them the right to have a say in the running of the country was not going to have much of an impact on how they were feeling. They felt disempowered and disconnected. As far as they were concerned politics wasn't for them and didn't affect their lives. Me and another youth worker, Danny, asked them what issues did affect them. We started to explain how politics can influence change in these areas and how young adults can influence political decisions both individually and as a collective.

The 2015 general election seemed a perfect time to get together a politics group and start to have conversations about issues that affected our community. Part of the work we did with the group focused on learning about the political system in the UK and on how the electoral system works. As the election got closer we hosted a TV-style debate at Manchester Metropolitan University with local candidates from the main parties so that young adults could ask any questions they wanted to. The young adults gave the parliamentary candidates a good grilling about issues affecting their education and future employment. It was great to see them so involved. Their voices were being heard and suddenly politics seemed to them to be more relevant and interesting.

We decided to build on the enthusiasm of our group to take some positive social action in the community. At that time we didn't need to look very far to find policies directly affecting young people in the area because Manchester City Council had just proposed cuts to youth work budgets. Again it was one of those times where the usual response is, 'That stinks, but what can we do?' Individually we can't do anything but together we can at least express how we feel about it and let the council know what an impact the new policy would have on our lives.

Together we worded a petition against the cuts, explaining how beneficial the Youth Fund is for young people in the area. More than 2,700 people from across the city signed a petition requesting the council to reconsider its decision. As a result, a number of the young people from M13 Youth Project and other youth initiatives in the area were invited to the council's scrutiny committee where they were able to raise their concerns about the proposed funding cuts.

In January 2015, Manchester City Council announced that it would reduce its cuts to the Youth and Play budget by £737,000 and committed to retaining the Youth Fund at its current level. For us it was a great victory because it showed the young people that politics does matter to their lives and that together people can make change happen.

15 An opportunity to love

Janet Morley

Janet Morley was one of the first volunteers at St Leonard's Hospice in York when it opened in 1985. During the next 30 years she took on a variety of roles, from care assistant to deputy chief executive. Janet was one of the founders of the National Association of Hospice Fundraisers and assisted setting up the Hospice National Retail Group. In 2014 she was presented with the Anne Norfolk Award for Lifetime Achievement in Fundraising by Hospice UK.

'And God is able to provide you with every blessing in abundance, so that by always having enough of everything, you may share abundantly in every good work' (2 Corinthians 9:8).

John Sentamu writes:

Is there such a thing as coincidence? The plots of so many films and books have depended on the idea of coincidence – of our blind unstructured life being given a pattern or a meaning by a 'coincidence' of events

On one level, Janet's story could seem like just one coincidence after another, with everything falling into place because of being in the right place at the right time. But, time and again, God shows us that there is no coincidence – only his plan. Was it coincidence that Jesus happened to be passing by when ten lepers needed to be healed? Was it coincidence that a boy had five loaves and two small fishes when the crowd needed to be fed?

There is a well-known saying that 'Our coincidences are God's opportunities'. God's purpose for each one of us is perfect and will be worked out – even if there are twists and turns along the way. For our loving Father in heaven makes the impossible possible.

Janet found that each new step in her life led seamlessly to the next opportunity, and each was a source of blessing. Let us always be ready to embrace each God-incident, and let God, who is able, 'provide us with every blessing in abundance.'

✠

The year I moved to York coincided with the climax of an appeal to build St Leonard's Hospice in York. I was looking for something to do so when it opened the following summer I joined the ranks of curious volunteers. I say curious because to be brutally honest, I first volunteered out of convenience. I was looking for something to occupy my time, the Hospice was local, and it felt exciting to be in at the beginning of something. As clichéd as it might sound, I like people and thought I'd enjoy that side of it. I didn't give too much thought to how I might feel when those same people died. It wasn't something that I'd ever had to think about because I'd never been with a friend or family member who was dying and I'd never seen a dead body. In that respect my choice of voluntary work was a steep learning curve.

My first experience of someone dying at the Hospice came as a shock to me. It's not the kind of thing you can leave at the office, so to speak. Of course, today lots of people who come into a hospice will go home again or to a nursing home. There may not be a cure for their illness but sometimes the Hospice can help to sort out the balance of medication so that a person can have a better quality of life in their final months. In the early days about 95 per cent of patients who came to the Hospice were terminally ill and would die while staying with us. It's not that I ever got used to it, but I came to appreciate what a tremendous privilege it is to be with someone on that final part of their life journey. It helped too to know that I wasn't alone in how I was feeling – I started with a large group of volunteers who were all new to hospice care and in that way we built up our own support network. We were always encouraged to talk about how we were feeling and other people were sensitive to who was feeling up or a little low on any particular day. There will always be some situations that hit us more acutely than others. For me, caring for a mum with two teenage children felt a bit too close to my life. Other staff recognised this and asked: 'Do you want to carry on or should I ask Mary to step-in instead?' In this way I felt supported by other volunteers and by staff every step of the way until suddenly I thought, I can do this work and I enjoy doing it. People would call us angels, but we're not. We're just ordinary men and women who love other people and realise what a great privilege it is to be given an opportunity to love in this way. There was a great sense of community among us and for me that is still the essence of the Hospice.

My first role was as a ward helper, which in practical terms meant turning up for a couple of hours in the afternoon and serving tea and cakes to patients and visitors. At the time my paid work was behind the counter of a high street bank, serving customers at lunch time. It fitted in neatly with school runs and looking after the children, but I knew it wasn't something I'd be interested in full-time. In contrast I was enjoying the volunteering and had only been doing it a matter of weeks when the Hospice started advertising for care assistants, so I applied and I was delighted to be offered the job. I'm not recommending that everybody goes and tries it but I always feel lucky to have been able to do that job as part of my working life. I got to experience such special moments, like holding the hand of a person during his or her last hours, because we would never leave someone alone at that time. It's almost one of the final things you can do for somebody. Often, when people know they are nearing the end of life, barriers come down and people talk about how they really feel. All being well, there is a need to not leave things unsaid and to be a part of that, to experience a person without the many artificial barriers we can place around ourselves, is a marvellous feeling.

As the Hospice expanded from 8 beds to 16, and later 20, the administration work involved could no longer be managed by volunteers alone. I knew I could do that type of work because after leaving school I'd worked for Leeds City Council as a management trainee and then careers officer. When a post was created at the Hospice for a paid administrative assistant I applied. For the first three months after getting the job I did both roles, working as an administrative assistant in the morning and a care assistant in the evening. However, it soon became clear that I would need to commit to one role or the other and although I loved the work as a care assistant my skills were more organisational. As a compromise I took on the administrative role and also went on what they call the bank, which meant if they were really desperate they would ask me to do a shift on the ward. It turned out that I'd do a shift about once a month and it made for a neat transition. The physical layout of the building also made the change easier for me because my workplace wasn't in a separate wing from the ward, and I still had that the contact with patients and their families, which I loved.

Being in when the Hospice was starting out meant that I did a bit of everything – one day I might be helping out with breakfasts in the kitchen, another I'd be writing salary cheques and then another I'd sit on reception for an hour. As time went on it became clear that somebody needed to coordinate the fundraising efforts – to keep people on-board and informed, and to make sure that they were doing any fundraising safely and within reasonable rules and guidelines. I said: 'I can do that,' and that is how I was appointed fundraising organiser. All my family and friends got involved helping out in some way. There was the support from the community as well, which has always been the essence of the Hospice. People might say, 'It's only £5' but if 100 people give us £5 that's £500 and pays for a bed.

From there, the job just grew and grew until suddenly there was a whole team of fundraisers. The good thing about hospices is that they have clearly defined geographical areas, so when raising money there is an unwritten rule that you don't run events in someone else's area. At the time when fundraising teams were small, sometimes not even made up of one full-time member of staff, the obvious thing to me was to ring neighbouring hospices and get in touch with their fundraisers. At first four of us from different hospices got together and started to share ideas – what had worked well, whilst being honest about what didn't. We learned so much from each other and the network grew from there to become a formal organisation: The National Association of Hospice Fundraisers.

I don't think anyone starts a job thinking they will be working in the same place 30 years later, but I felt as the organisation grew so did I. When I walked through those doors offering to volunteer I could never have imagined what my job would become. When I retired, in 2015, my role had changed again, and I was deputy chief executive. I constantly think about how fortunate I was and my peers at other hospices would remind me of that too. Sometimes I'd worry that I didn't deserve the opportunities that came my way; that perhaps it was just that no one dare say no to me, but I don't think it was like that. There was definitely an element of being in the right place at the right time, but at the same time when an opportunity came up I thought – grab this with both hands and give it your best shot. I was always happy to give new things a go because I always felt supported. That support enabled me to give a commitment that I'd never experienced in my working life before. I was brought up in a strong Methodist family during the 1950s. My father and grandfather were both Boys' Brigade officers. I later became a Boys' Brigade officer and my husband did too. We were always doing something for someone else; it was just how we were. To have that opportunity within my paid job was really special and I always got so much pleasure from working there. Everyone around me got involved – my mum, my husband, my children, my friends – the Hospice was a big part of all of our lives.

It was no surprise when I reached a certain age that I was going to move on, but it was still a difficult decision to make. There was nothing scientific in my thinking. My husband had retired three years earlier. He said: 'You can get a bus pass when you're 62', so in my head that became the date I'd retire. I gave one year's notice of my leaving but it was only as the time edged nearer and I was counting weeks rather than months that it started to feel real. People were talking about events coming up that didn't include me anymore and it was like I'd stepped outside.

I didn't want a big send off when I left and everyone understood why. Leaving after that length of time – it's a wrench. At the end of my last day, I placed my keys on the Chief Executive Martyn Callaghan's desk and he said: 'I won't say anything because it'll upset you.' I pulled on my coat, picked up my bag and walked out.

As I got to the door someone spoke to me and I crumbled. 'Go on, you'll be fine,' she said. It was lovely to hear, but walking up the drive to my car I couldn't hide my heartbreak. Thinking back, I probably shouldn't have driven home, but I did and thankfully my husband was sensitive. He made me a cup of tea and I cried. When the finality of it hit me, I felt the loss as a physical pain that lasted weeks. At the same time I didn't want to go back because I knew retiring was the right decision for me, for my family and for the Hospice. I'd seen lots of people work on because they didn't have a choice to retire, and then die soon after they were able to retire. I was fortunate to have the choice. Fundraising is a very physical job and I'm not as energetic as I was 30 years ago. The Hospice needed a fresh pair of eyes, someone to come in with new energy, but while I knew all of this, I missed the people and my work and it felt like a big hole in my chest, the pain of which took me by surprise. You might say: why didn't I go back as a volunteer? I did have a strange dilemma about it, but to me that felt unfair on the other people working there. I had to let them get on, and to do things in the way they choose to do them.

About eight weeks after I left the Chief Executive rang and asked if I'd like to meet my successor. 'I'd love to', I said. We met in a nearby café and recognised each other straight away. We chatted for a while about the Hospice and different things, then I said: 'The last thing I want you to feel, is that you have to be the new Janet. You have to be yourself, so don't think that you need to stick with things just because that's what I used to do.' She took it in the manner in which I had intended it and we got on really well. As I was leaving, I said: 'If you don't want to contact me again, that's fine, but if you do I'm here as well.' It felt comfortable and I could sense myself feeling more settled. I suppose I'd been worrying about who was going to do the job, what they'd be like, will they still look after people in the same way, all those things which of course she has done. She's doing a cracking job and knowing that helps tremendously. She's rung a couple of times since and it's always lovely for me to be asked, but equally I'm glad that it's not every day.

I joined the Hospice just as it was opening and left having overseen a complete refurbishment. It was a great way to finish because it felt like I was completing a circle. Lots of things have changed in that 30 years since I joined. People are more aware of the work of hospices, treatments have improved, facilities have expanded, but in essence the Hospice is the same. At its heart it's about people, and people are still the same – their needs haven't changed. Sometimes we can get caught up in life and put off opportunities that may never come our way again. Working at the Hospice taught me not to put things off, to make the best of opportunities that come my way, and to live life to the full, as far as I possibly can. We're all human, so sometimes I forget my good intentions for a while, but being in a hospice always reminded me to savour every minute.

16 'If you lose the memory you lose the lesson'

Tiki Raumati

Archdeacon Tiki Raumati is Kaumātua of the Taranaki Cathedral Church of St Mary in New Zealand. He is descended from the nineteenth-century Maori teacher and prophet, Te Whiti o Rongomai of Parihaka, and for many years has acted as a bridge between the Maori and Pakeha worlds.

'So if anyone is in Christ, there is a new creation: everything old has passed away; see, everything has become new! All this is from God, who reconciled us to himself through Christ, and has given us the ministry of reconciliation; that is, in Christ God was reconciling the world to himself, not counting their trespasses against them, and entrusting the message of reconciliation to us'
(2 Corinthians 5:17-19).

John Sentamu writes:

20 years ago, Archbishop Desmond Tutu was appointed as chair of the Truth and Reconciliation Commission set up in South Africa, to help the new Government find a peaceful way forward after the pain and injustice of the apartheid years. Honouring people's stories and making space for repentance and forgiveness cleared the way for a new kind of country to develop. Around 40 Truth and Reconciliation Commissions have been set up in countries across the world as nations seek to deal with their wounded history.

Jesus said, *'Blessed are the peacemakers, for they will be called the children of God'* (Matthew 5:9). Tiki Raumati's story shows how his desire for peace, coupled with a love of truth and justice, have enabled him to help the Maori and Paheka communities to face their past and begin the process of reconciliation, forgiveness and love together.

'You will know the truth, and the truth will make you free' (John 8:32), said Jesus to 'those who had believed in him'. Through his death and resurrection, Jesus Christ reconciled us to the Father and to one another. So let us never be afraid to look at the truth of our lives, and be ever set free to make peace with our brothers and sisters.

✢

All my life, throughout Maoridom, I have heard: *'He aha te mea nui? Maku e ki atu, He tangata, He tangata, He tangata!'* In English it means, 'What is the greatest thing in the world? It is People, People, People!' There is no reference to M ori or Pakeha (the Maori term for New Zealanders of European descent). Neither is there any mention of ethnicity, colour, culture, creed, or whatever distinctions you might like to add to the list - just people! He Tangata – it doesn't matter where we are from, we are important because we are made in the likeness and image of God. You can separate us into as many different classes as you like, but everyone, whoever they are,

comes into this world the same way and we all leave the same
way too. We are all part of that human condition and are all
fallible.

My father always used to say: 'Peace, peace at all costs.
It doesn't matter what it costs, it is peace!' He learned that
from his father, and my grandfather learned it from his father
before him. When I think about what that old Maori tradition
means I imagine a crisp, white sheet. Spill a drop of blood on
that sheet and you'd see it from a mile away – there's no hiding
it. My ancestors didn't want me to fight, they wanted me to
remain myself; perfectly myself, with my heart as pure as the
snow on the top of a mountain, symbolised by the plume of
my headdress.

In British and some other cultures, a white feather is used to
symbolise cowardice. My Maori ancestors liked to turn things
that were bad into something good. So, for us the white feather
became a symbol of peace at all costs. We'd wear the feather,
as white as a snow-capped mountain, on our brow and hold
our heads up high. We were to wear that peace emblem on
the top of our heads for the whole world to see, and whatever
happened we were not to soil it.

When our ancestors spoke of soiling they meant no killing.
My hapu or sub-tribe, Kaitangata, literally means 'eat people'.
In other words, my ancestors were once cannibals. Te Whiti
o Rongomai, a Maori teacher and prophet who had a deep
knowledge of the Christian faith, told the people of the time:
'Stop! No more killing, no more eating.' When he said killing,
he didn't just mean no eating of flesh. He meant no more killing
no matter who it is, for whatever reason.

Te Whiti lived during the Musket Wars of the nineteenth
century. His teachings were the main reason why when the
European invaders came, the 2000 Maori inhabitants put up
no resistance. Instead they greeted the men with hospitality,
an idea which probably also came from the Bible to feed your
enemy, not soil them. In Parihaka, where Te Whiti was living,
the Maori people laid out food and the invading army rode
their blooming horses over the tucker that was served up for

them. My ancestors kept their heads high – peace at all costs. Why look down, when you're in the poo?

I was born the fifteenth child in a family of 18 children. Being the last of the brothers I think my mother's main hope for me was that I wouldn't get into trouble. My father was born sighted but lost his sight later in life. By the time I was born my father was blind and being his youngest son I was appointed as his guide. You could say that for many years I was my father's eyes. Whenever we rode into town he'd sit me between his legs in the gig and I'd drive. Sometimes I'd get called a little so and so, quite rudely, but I hardened to it. There was no good chasing something I knew was going to cause trouble so I sort of rode it out and accepted it. As my father would tell me: 'Whatever they throw at you treat it with kindness.' In other words, 'If you must kill people, do it with kindness and not with the sword'.

I guess I broke the mould when I joined the army and trained to be a soldier. It wasn't that I chose it; for young men military service was compulsory and although my father had passed away when I signed up, I also remembered him telling me: 'Take care to obey the law of the land, because if you don't you're in trouble.' The first time I came home in uniform was for three days' leave. The bus stopped at our gate and I hopped out to see my mother waiting for me. 'Don't you come in here yet,' she said and continued to lecture me about all the peace and reconciliation that had gone before in our family. When she'd finished she said: 'You can come in, son, but I just wanted to tell you what your father would have done, all right? Now, take those boots off.'

After my compulsory service I finished my schooling and at the age of 21, I told my mother I was thinking of becoming a priest. 'I'm fairly certain your father would've approved,' she told me, 'If you choose this path, you won't earn much but I will support you.' I was ordained as a minister of the Anglican Church on 30 November 1965 in the oldest stone church in New Zealand, known then as St Mary's Church, New Plymouth. The church was full of people, except for five empty pews at the front. I heard the Bishop ask Canon Wii Huata of the Maori Mission, 'Whose seats are those?' and the reply that they belonged to my family. Our procession continued until we reached the altar, then just as our ceremony was about to begin I heard my mother cry out in Maori. My hair stood on end, this is my mother! What is she doing? Until that moment I'd been thinking to myself how beautiful it all was – the sung litany, the stone building. Now my only thought was, what is happening? My mother was standing there with my family behind her. What she was saying was all new to me and it wasn't until she completed her call that I calmed down. She said: 'Son, now that you have joined this religion we have come to offer you our support. However, I want you to know so that you'll never forget – this building was used to store the ammunition that was used to kill your ancestors.'

We went through the service and afterwards a lot of people were asking me, 'What's this Maori thing that they did?' I wanted to leave it, but my brothers and sisters kept at me to explain, so I told people: 'Hey, come on, I think we are starting on the right foot. This is the cost of the gospel of Christ – the truth will set us free.'

What my mother was referring to in her call was that during the Taranaki wars of the 1860s St Mary's became a garrison church, the church for the settlers and the army. To this day, 19th century British army hatchments (diamond-shaped plaques bearing regimental coats of arms) line the walls of the nave. A pain like this resonates widely through generations. Many Pakeha are embarrassed by them now but I always say that we shouldn't remove these hatchments completely. To do that would be to remove the history; if you remove the history you lose the memory, and if you lose the memory you lose the lesson.

Before the day of my ordination I never knew anything about that particular part of the history of our church. It was always there, but it was never spoken of. Knowing it now didn't give me any vicious thoughts towards the church. My immediate reaction was, there is nothing wrong with the church, we are the problem, not the church. The foundation of the church is set, but we the people have come and made a mess of it. I still think that today.

As I got older I learned things that happened within my family that had been slightly hidden away. I remember seeing my grandma and thinking, oh gosh, that's a Pakeha woman, because she was fair as fair can be. My dad was a bit naughty in the respect that he let my mother refer to him as being in a different 'station', you might say, class. Then I found out my father was just as bad, he had all this European blood in him but he couldn't tell me, Tiki Raumati. Thank you very much for the nice name my great grandfather gave our father, 'Raumati', but in fact he was a 'Damon' and those names came from real people. So there was that kind of hidden history as well of the first integration of Maori and European peoples. I woke up pretty quickly to realise that I'm part of that too; otherwise I would never be who I am today. This is why I keep saying, know who you are and accept who you are, because when you know yourself I think you cope much better in life.

Te Whiti used the story of the speckled potato, the result of cross-pollination between the Maori potato - kumara - with a red skin and a European potato. Speckled potatoes are nice, hard, beautiful spuds. Te Whiti used this analogy to show that in due course intermarriage would force us to address our differences. It's another way of saying, love conquers all. In my own family for example, my wife, Wilma is English. People say to me, 'You got a Pakeha wife!' I say, 'Yeah, and she's wonderful. I'm the luckiest man alive.' It's the same with my daughter; when we were fighting the Germans she decided to marry one. So my grandchildren are German. Am I going to cut them off because they are German? Of course not, they are beautiful and they are my grandchildren. The way I see it, all children are our children, and that's how we should view them. Our children signify our new beginning, but we can't find the kind of future we dream of if we don't face the past honestly and with real understanding. That's what my mother was saying in her call. She was supporting my being ordained but at the same time telling me to not forget the history, because history informs how we deal with relationships in the present and how we move into the future.

In March 2010, St Mary's New Plymouth was consecrated by the Archbishop of York, Dr John Sentamu, as a fully-fledged cathedral – the first new Anglican Cathedral in New Zealand in more than 80 years. I was the first Maori priest to be ordained there and when I was installed as New Zealand's first Cathedral Kaumatua (Maori elder) I was still the only Maori priest to be ordained there, so there is still reconciliatory work for me to do.

The Maori people have always commemorated the invasion of Parihaka by Crown troops more than 130 years ago, but 2010 was the first time the service was held at St Mary's Church. The consecration of the new Cathedral was to be the starting point for reconciliation. Early in the service I presented Bishop Philip Richardson with a gift of a cope and mitre. The cope had a shield of feathers on the back symbolising peace at all costs. It was a visible sign that Bishop Philip was taking on my people's history – the whiteness, don't soil it. In doing so he was saying to his people, we've got to clean this up and we've got to keep it clean. For as long as we keep it clean and our heads raised towards the mountain, we'll be all right.

Bishop Philip spoke of his hopes for a new beginning and how he prayed that St Mary's would now become a cathedral for all the people of Taranaki. During the service he said to me: 'In a few days we commemorate the beginning of a conflict that gave birth to the great movement centred on Parihaka.

'This Church stood, perhaps inevitably, on one side of that conflict. This has been a source of deep alienation for many of your people, and you recall clearly your mother's words in this very church.

'For that alienation and for that breach of trust I am deeply sorry, both personally but also as Bishop of Taranaki.

'The commitment I make today on behalf of myself and my successors is that the people of this Church, together with the Dean and myself, will honestly face the past, so that with true and honest understanding we may build a new future. We will deal with the signs and symbols of one part of the story.

'As Cathedral Kaumatua we are not asking you to do the work for us, but by your grace and generosity of vision allow us to do this work in your presence ... so that in the future this Cathedral may be a place for all, and a place where Tangata Whenua may have an appropriate role in the governance and oversight of this Church.

'My dream is that this may truly be a Cathedral for all the people of Taranaki without impediment, a place of peace and reconciliation based on justice and understanding.'

That too is my dream. I think of my own life – my marriage to my English Rose, Wilma, and our families. Maori or Pakeha, you can't separate us now, we are here to stay and our two tribes are only going to get closer whether we like it or not. Our cathedral belongs to all God's people and if it does not, we are in big trouble.

Te Whiti left this message to the people of Te Atiawa which is written on the plaque of dedication for our cathedral: 'Let our grandchildren and those yet unborn, give praise for what we have left to hang on to'.

Peace - or, as we say in Maori language, paimarie at all costs!

17 A forgiving spirit

Maureen Greaves

Maureen Greaves received a British Empire Medal in the Queen's Birthday Honours list of 2015 in recognition of her services to the community in north Sheffield. On Christmas Eve 2012 her husband, Alan, was brutally murdered as he walked to church where he was due to play the organ at midnight mass. Following her loss, Maureen has continued the charitable work she did alongside Alan for many years, including running the charity shop they started in their garage, which had opened in new premises just three weeks before Alan was killed.

> **'In him was life, and the life was the light of all people. The light shines in the darkness, and the darkness did not overcome it' (John 1:4–5).**

John Sentamu writes:

Maureen's story is a painful picture of a world living in darkness where, even on one of the holiest and most joyful nights of the year, senseless evil can strike. She and her beloved husband had been loving and serving God together in their community for 40 years. How could she now deal with his brutal and gratuitous murder on the way to church on Christmas Eve?

Maureen found, as others have found, that forgiveness is impossible in our own strength. Only the power of God's unending forgiveness, working through us, can make it possible.

Forgiveness seems to many an illogical and incredible response to the cruelty of the world, but for those who ask God's help, it becomes the only way out of the darkness. The Holy Spirit breathes God's forgiveness into us and lifts us out of the mire of despond – planting our feet on the solid ground which is Christ Jesus. It is amazing healing.

On the first day of Christmas, Jesus Christ was born into a world of spiritual darkness and sin. He is the light which came into the world to banish the shadows. And the deepest darkness of the world did not overcome it. His light is still shining – even in the darkest times in our lives. If we turn to his light, the darkness will never overcome us. His light will warm, guide and refine us like pure gold. Come, Holy Spirit, come!

✠

When you've been passionately in love with someone there's a sense in which you want to say goodbye and I still find it difficult that I didn't get that opportunity with Alan. I was 21 years old when we met. I remember seeing him for the first time. We were in college together training to be residential child care officers. I was already in the classroom when Alan walked in and introduced himself to the lecturer. I didn't know anything about him at that time, he was a complete stranger, yet I felt an instant attraction to him that was so powerful the thought even crossed my mind that this was the person I wanted to marry. I wasn't sure what to do about these feelings, so I decided to pray about it. As it was, our introduction happened quite naturally. Later that day we were going on a visit as part of our course. I was last to get on the bus and the only seat left was next to Alan. On the journey we drove past the church I attended and as we chatted I pointed and said: 'I go to that church.'

'I go to church too,' he said, and in my heart that extra piece of information sealed our connection. After that I just waited for him to make a move, which didn't happen as soon as I might have liked. There were gaps where we didn't see each other for months at a time while on work placements. When I later asked Alan why it took him so long to ask me to go on a date he said: 'I was so in love with you, I wanted to do it all properly somehow. All this coming and going on different placements and not quite knowing where we were, it didn't feel right. I wanted to wait until we settled down into a better routine'. Six weeks from our first date Alan asked me to marry him. It was Christmas and I was delighted to be his wife.

For our first two and a half years of marriage we worked together at a reception centre where children from babies to 18-year-olds were cared for while the court made a decision about their future. I left the centre when I got pregnant with our first child Emma, and we went on to have three more children born close together: Martin, Peter and Alison. Peter has mild learning difficulties. Martin has Prader-Willi syndrome, which is a rare genetic condition that happens by chance. In very simple language it means that his glands don't function properly and he hasn't got any chemicals to tell him that he's eaten and it put him in a vulnerable position because he'd go with anyone who offered him food. When you've got two children with disabilities you need to make sure everything is okay with them, so we chose for me to give up work and stay at home until they were all a bit more grown up.

About the same time that we started our family Alan left his job in residential care and went to work as a social worker.

He was later made a senior social worker but decided not to go above that because of his strong commitment to our family and the church. He became a Reader in the Church of England and he also had a big commitment to music, which he absolutely loved. Alan came from a musical family. His mother was a piano teacher and also played the violin and clarinet. His father played the cello and flute, and Alan played piano, guitar and clarinet. He was also a beautiful singer and our house was always filled with music. I enjoy singing but I never shared that same musical talent I so admired in Alan. Our upbringings had been very different, in that Alan was the only child of a middle-class family whereas I was one of seven children brought up in a working-class home, squeezed in a two-up two-down terraced house in Attercliffe. In many ways you might say it was an attraction of opposites, but those superficial differences never bothered us, because it is true to say we were passionately in love. While we had our rows, where he might have said the sky's red and I would have said, no it's blue, our love never wavered.

Working together, as well as all the commitments we shared, really did bond us. Although we had stopped working together at the centre, for the next 40 years we were always involved in voluntary projects with the church and surrounding community. Doing this type of work you meet a wide variety of people in different circumstances and get some understanding of their needs without them having to ask for help directly. For example, I once visited a woman who, when I went to sit down, said: 'Oh, don't sit there. We did have a throw to cover it, but the dog chewed it and there's no way we'll ever be able to replace it.' Or I'd often hear: 'I'm sorry I can't offer you a biscuit, we don't have any in the house and I don't get my money until next week.' We started using our garage to collect food, clothes and furniture so that when we came across people they could come and have a look and take what they needed. After a while the need grew so big that we asked our church if there was any way we could open a proper shop, full time. A shop unit became available on our road and, once we got an agreement to go ahead, Alan brought together a group of people and devoted a lot of time setting it up ready to open, by getting the furniture and the shelving in and all sorts of things.

Everyone involved was a volunteer from the church or the community so in some ways we were all hoofing it a little bit, seeing what worked and what didn't. It's a shop, pretty much like most charity shops, but in addition it's got a little sitting room where people can come and have a coffee. There's also a food bank and a washing machine, because people often used to say to me: 'Please mind the pile of clothes, the washing machine's broken and I haven't got the money to get it mended and there's no laundrette round here.'

The shop opened on 1 December 2012 and that Christmas we had a lot to look forward to as a family. Our daughter, Alison, who works as a missionary in Mozambique, was coming home with the four-year-old twins she adopted as babies. We hadn't seen them for two years and it was the twins' first Christmas in the UK so everything was exciting for them – they'd never seen a Christmas tree all lit up. On Christmas Eve all our children were with us at home. It was a lovely evening, singing, laughing, looking at old photos and reminiscing. Alan always played the organ at the midnight service, I stayed home with the children and we all went to church together on Christmas morning. Even after the children grew up that was our tradition and this Christmas Eve was no different to any other in that respect. Alan set off at his usual time and after a few minutes came back. 'Oh, Maureen', he said, 'it's a bitterly cold night. I've come back for my hat'. Now you could reflect and say what if he hadn't come back for his hat, but I don't think like that because I know life is full of 'what ifs?'. He did come back for his hat, we kissed, I said: 'Don't be late love,' and out he went. There was nothing special about the ending. It wasn't a romantic ending in that sense.

After Alan left for church I went to bed as usual but I didn't sleep; I always stayed awake until he came back in. It's just one of those strange quirks you do as a couple. It must have been perhaps midnight-ish, although I didn't look at the clock, when there was a knock at the door. I opened it to see two policemen. 'Are you Mrs Greaves? Can we come in?'

'Your husband's had an accident.'

'Oh, where is he?'

'Northern General. He's had an accident to his head, would you like us to take you down now?'

'Oh, no, I'll go and get dressed. Let me go and fetch him. It's Christmas day tomorrow. I'm leading the service and Alan is preaching so I really want to make sure he's all right'.

Our daughter Emma is a dispatcher at South Yorkshire police, which means that she takes distress calls and works on major incidents. She'd been working that morning and her shift finished at 2pm. Had she been on the later shift, she would most likely have taken the initial call. I thank God she wasn't working that evening, but even as the police officers came into our kitchen, possibly because of the word, 'accident,' I didn't think there was anything seriously wrong.

Hearing the door, Alison came out of the bedroom: 'What's happening?'

'Oh don't worry, you go back to bed. Your dad's had an accident to his head. I'll be fine'.

I got dressed and when I went back into the kitchen, the police officer said again: 'Can we take you?'

I got in the car, quite at ease and I sang carols all the way to the hospital. When I got there I went to the reception and was told: 'The consultant is still with Alan, would you mind sitting in the waiting room, he'll be ready for you in a few minutes'. I went into the waiting room still quite at ease but realised as soon as the consultant walked in that something was very wrong. I could see it in his whole demeanour. He appeared haggard and looked quite awful. He pulled a chair close towards me and sat down. 'I'm very sorry to tell you that it appears to us that your husband has been attacked,' he said. 'He's been attacked very brutally on his head, a very vicious attack.'

'Is Alan dying?' I asked.

'I don't think he'll live.'

My first thought was, Oh, God, no. Not an ending like this. Then my mind didn't work properly because I thought that Alan would be able to speak to me and I said, 'Please just take me to him. I want to say goodbye'.

When I got there the trauma team was with Alan and that's a lot of people. They all lowered their heads and no one spoke. Even in my shock I could recognise how stricken everyone looked at what they were dealing with. I couldn't recognise Alan. His head had swollen up to proportions that had almost distorted his features, and he was covered in cuts and blood. I knew then that he was going to die. I walked over to his bed. There were wires and tubes all over his body and up his nose, keeping him breathing on an artificial ventilator. I took his hand. That part of him I did recognise. As much as I didn't want to believe it was Alan lying there, it was him.

'Can I please ring my daughters to come?' I asked.

As soon as I heard Alison's voice the tears came and I couldn't get my words out. The consultant took the phone from me.

Alan was transferred to the specialist brain injury unit at the Royal Hallamshire. I travelled in the ambulance with him, and the doctor asked Emma and Alison to meet us there. I waited in the area by the lifts and when I saw them we all cried. How do you tell your daughters something like that? We were shown to a family waiting room and it was probably about 3am when a consultant came to see us. 'I can't tell you this in any other way,' he said, 'this is one of the worst head injuries we've ever come across. If Alan should in any way survive this and live he will only live on a ventilator for the rest of his life and will never be able to do anything for himself.' The two girls almost screamed out their agony. The scans showed quite clearly that Alan's skull was battered and that splinters of his skull were going into his brain. On the right hand side of his head, just above his right eyebrow there was a big opening where something had penetrated Alan's skin, gone through his flesh, into the bone and broken the bone and pulled it out. A piece of his skull, the size of two digits of your little finger, was found on the ground at the scene of the crime. There was a steady flow of medical staff coming to see Alan and do tests, and when they read the results it was always with a shake of the head. Alan was dying and I knew I needed to tell our sons.

Emma made the calls for me early on Christmas morning and agreed to bring the boys to see their dad the next day. At about 9am all my brothers and sisters and our nephews and nieces started arriving. We couldn't fit everyone into the waiting room. We asked if we could go in one by one as a family to say goodbye to Alan. At lunch time our vicar came and we had Christmas Communion. Then at tea time everyone went home, our daughters went to get a cup of tea and there was just me, Alan and a nurse. I sat next to him and I took his hand. If Alan could've spoken to me, I'm as convinced as any person can be that he would've said two things. I've loved you passionately always and don't give yourself permission to hate – forgive them.

When you come together in a marriage you bring your strengths and your weaknesses. My weakness was that I could be unforgiving. A few months into our marriage we'd had an argument and I'd done some sulking. Alan, having no brothers or sisters had never experienced this behaviour and afterwards he asked, 'What was all that about?' We talked about it and he said: 'We must never give ourselves permission to behave like this you know. It's not honouring to God. Together we need to think about how we do behave'. I must say that I don't think I ever didn't forgive Alan for anything he might have said or done, or my children, but I would walk on the other side of the road if I saw somebody I didn't like or who had hurt me in some way. It was something in me that I had to work on quite strongly and something that kept coming back and nipping at me.

Holding Alan's hand I asked God, 'What am I going to do with all of this? How am I going to manage without Alan? How am I going to get through this?' As I was praying I realised with quite a force that this was going to be a murder investigation, somebody had done this to Alan. I couldn't go back to living with unforgiveness, when I'd worked all my life to nurture a forgiving spirit. I prayed for God to give me the ability to fully forgive whoever had murdered Alan, now and forever, because I knew that one day if they were caught I would see them. I asked for God to take Alan's murderers into his hands so that I didn't have to carry them. In a sense I was asking to be set free, because I have four children to look after, and I didn't want us to live the rest of our lives bound to this murder. I didn't want this murder to destroy us. I wanted us to be able to continue our lives knowing that God will deal with it, both justly and in his love and mercy.

Alan died at 10.30pm on 27 December 2012. The following day we walked down the street as a family to see where the attack happened. There was a white tent keeping the crime scene safe and lots of people had left flowers and crosses on the railings nearby. As we approached people came towards us from all directions to offer their condolences, crying and hugging us. There were so many people that it took more than an hour and a half to walk a short distance. It felt like the whole community was in shock.

I went back to work the following February because at the time not only was I very heartbroken over Alan's loss but there was a heavy police investigation and it did me some good to come away from it and spend some time in a very different situation. In July 2013 Jonathan Bowling, aged 22, admitted attacking Alan with a pickaxe handle and was jailed for a minimum of 25 years. His step-brother, Ashley Foster, also aged 22, was found guilty of manslaughter for his part in the attack and received a nine year sentence. My prayer has always been that while in prison they will have time to reflect on their lives, on what they have done, and to come out different men. By God's grace our family has not been ruined by anger towards them. We came home after the trial and said it's okay to leave them in God's hands now, and it's been that way for us ever since.

I've carried on with the community work that Alan and I had started together. The shop has developed a lot over the past three years. We've added a furniture garage, a job club, Citizens Advice, a micro savings and lending scheme, a food bank, and we've recently started a community allotment because we thought it would be nice to encourage people to grow food as well. Alan would be delighted to see how it's thriving.

There isn't a day when I don't miss him. It isn't that I have to purposely think of Alan, he's just there in my thoughts and in my heart. I've a feeling that that will probably always be so. Life isn't the same and I miss Alan terribly, but God is at work and by his grace I've been able to carry on and live a fulfilled life.

Patricia Mutangili

Patricia Mutangili is a tea farmer from the slopes of Mount Kenya. She is one of 8,500 farmers who sell tea to the Ndima tea factory, which supplies tea used in the Traidcraft range. She is known to her neighbours as Mama Fairtrade because of her efforts to promote Fairtrade to other tea farmers both within Kenya and worldwide.

'Happy is everyone who fears the LORD, who walks in his ways. You shall eat the fruit of the labour of your hands; you shall be happy, and it shall go well with you' (Psalm 128:1-2).

John Sentamu writes:

God our Father created a world of great beauty and great bounty; where there was food and work for all; where love and justice reigned and the man and the woman he made were blessed. Since the disobedience of Adam, when sin came into the world, this balance has been broken and inequality and injustice have been allowed to flourish. *'Grasping, idolatry, enmities, strife, jealousy, anger, quarrels, dissensions, factions, envy, and things like these pollute God's world'* (Galatians 5:19-21). They are insidious.

The Psalmist who wrote Psalm 128 knew that the right balance between people and creation could only be achieved if human beings feared the Lord. This is not the kind of fear of an oppressor who will deal out harsh treatment, but the wholesome fear and awe which recognises the authority and power of God and obeys his will for his people. Because God is the God of love, joy, peace, and justice.

If we acknowledge his power and the rightness of his plans for us, and if we live our lives according to his plan, then we will be blessed with life in all its fullness and 'all manner of thing will be well for us'.

Mama Fairtrade's love of justice, and her readiness to follow each new path that the Lord showed her, have brought great joy and blessing not only to her, but to all those she serves through her work.

✠

More than 50 years ago my father planted 6,500 tea bushes in the rich volcanic soil of Mount Kenya, where the high altitude and equatorial location allows harvesting of good quality leaves all year round. For many years I picked the leaves by hand. I'd start early in the morning when the tea was still wet with dew and work until late in the afternoon. From the top of each plant I'd pluck two leaves and a bud – take any more than that and the quality diminishes. It means that as a tea picker you can cover a lot of ground in one day, filling basket after basket with fresh leaves. On average I would collect about 20 kilos of leaves a day and I'd do that job for six days a week, Monday to Saturday, all year round whatever the weather.

In Kenya, most of the tea is picked by women. I don't know why that is, but it is what usually happens. However, although women are the ones who pick the tea it is unusual for them to become tea farmers, I am one of the few. Usually in our culture it is the sons who inherit farming land from their parents. When my father decided to share his land he was unusual in that he treated his sons and daughters equally. One of my sisters and two of my brothers said that they didn't want to be farmers, so my father's bushes were shared between the remaining six of us.

In 2003, much to the surprise of many of my neighbours, I became a tea farmer, owning 1,000 bushes, stretching across half an acre of land. I was aged 38 and a single mother of two children. I had been married but I left my husband because of his abusive behaviour and moved with our two children into my parents' house. Some time after we split my husband died and I never remarried.

My father had given me a wonderful opportunity for me and my children, but while I knew about picking tea, there was a lot more I had to learn if I was going to make it as a farmer. First I had to register with the nearest tea factory in order to be able to sell the tea. Once the tea leaves had been picked I needed to arrange for them to be taken to a collection centre, where they would be weighed before delivery to a factory where the leaves would undergo a series of processes – withering, cutting, tearing, curling, fermenting, drying and sorting – before being packaged ready for sale. Getting through each of these stages wasn't enough on its own; there were other hurdles to jump. For me to sell my leaves I also needed to get a certification of quality from the International Organization for Standardisation, ISO. At first I wasn't sure what I needed to do to get this stamp of approval, but I told myself, it will be very simple, all of these other farmers are doing it, I'll just take a step to ask what I need to do.

It was in learning about the ISO that I first heard about a body called Fairtrade. At the time there were about 150 small farmers supplying leaves to the tea factory. This group of farmers formed a committee at the Tea Collection Centre to represent farmers and their needs to the factory. The manager of the factory told us about this scheme that was about getting better prices for our tea, better working conditions and fair terms of trade for farmers and workers. Everyone agreed that it sounded like a good scheme, but then the manager said that she wanted to train some of the farmers in Fairtrade practices so that we could become trainers and train the other farmers. At that point most of the farmers said that this Fairtrade was too difficult to understand. Perhaps I didn't think this because for me at that time everything about the farming aspect of tea was new, so when I heard the manager say this, I quickly volunteered. I was interested to learn and I thought that maybe Fairtrade would give everyone involved in the process a chance, tea pickers and farmers.

In many ways volunteering was the easy bit. Once I'd been selected I realised the responsibility I was taking on. If I was going to train other farmers I needed to know what I was doing, so before I went along for the training I started searching for Fairtrade on the internet and learning as much as I could about it. The more I read, the more I thought that this could be a good thing for us. As well as receiving a guaranteed minimum price for our product that would enable some stability for us as farmers, we would also be paid an additional Fairtrade premium which would go into a communal fund that we could use for improving education, housing, roads and medical facilities in our community. I didn't understand how it would work at that point, but it sounded exciting. I thought perhaps we might use some of these funds to help the tea pickers to learn new skills so that they had options. I remember as a tea picker sometimes thinking, I don't want to keep picking tea, day in and day out. I didn't want other women to feel like that, to feel that all they had to rely on was tea, to wake up in the morning and think, I must go and pick tea because there is nothing else I can do.

After I had completed the training, a special dinner was held for all the farmers in the region where a committee was elected to represent us. Although new to farming, because I had this new knowledge about Fairtrade I was one of those elected and shortly afterwards I was made chair of the committee. I recognised that if we were going to get the tea from our factory certificated as Fairtrade then we needed to get all the farmers on board. People don't like change, but I was sure that if other farmers understood the benefits then they would want to get involved too.

I organised a two day road show to help raise awareness among the other farmers in a way they could understand, and I took a comedian with me because I thought if we entertained as well as educated we might have a better chance of being heard. On the first day we went from village to village talking about Fairtrade, what it was and how it could help small farmers like us. I told them there were also social benefits of being certified by Fairtrade and asked what they might like to do with those funds. Many of them told me if it was possible they would like to have concrete benches at the collection centre on which they could spread the leaves from their baskets, because this surface would be cooler than the wooden benches and could stop the tea fermenting before it got to the factory where fermentation should take place. This was very important for farmers because early fermentation compromised quality. When I said it could be possible to pay for concrete benches with a Fairtrade premium the farmers were very happy and began getting excited by the idea of Fairtrade. On the second day of the road show, people were on the streets waiting for us to tell them more about it. As we approached they began shouting 'Mama Fairtrade', and the name stuck.

The benefits of Fairtrade were becoming clear to farmers, but ensuring that all farms met the criteria necessary to achieve a Fairtrade certificate was more challenging. Child labour was something that many farmers didn't realise was unacceptable. Every Saturday children would go to pick tea, either on their parent's or neighbour's farms. They would do the same when they were out of school for holiday, so every August, April and December children would be working on farms, any wages usually being collected by their parents. When we realised that we couldn't do that anymore because it was child labour, we put up notices up in the tea collection centre making it clear that we had a new policy. No child was allowed in the tea factory or the tea collection centre and no child was to be on the farm picking tea. Slowly the parents agreed to this until every farmer complied with the standards. It wasn't just children who benefitted, all the workers did. Before the farms had Fairtrade standards, tea pickers would work for ten or eleven hours a day, often without a break. Now tea is only picked between 7am and 4pm. No picker works for longer than eight hours and all workers have regular breaks.

Firewood is burned to provide the heat to dry the tea and so as you can imagine we use a lot of firewood in the area. Nobody thought anything about how we sourced the wood until in 2012 we began to notice that frost was damaging our tea, something we had never had any problems with before. I learned that the frost damage was most likely linked to deforestation in the area, which was causing climate change, but I wasn't sure what we could do about it. Fairtrade helped me to get a baseline survey on climate change and a risks and opportunities assessment on our tea catchment area. Now I had the data to show what was happening, my job was to go back to all the farmers I had spoken to about the economic and social benefits of Fairtrade and begin to raise awareness of the environmental benefits, with the aim of encouraging farmers to plant new trees to replace those cut for firewood.

I was chair of the committee for six years and feel blessed to be able to be a Fairtrade tea farmer encouraging others along the way. When I look back and think how far we have come, this has all been made possible because of Fairtrade. Now we have better employment, better facilities for housing and storing the tea, we have time off from work so our living improves and our children are educated in schools. We have developed more water-harvesting projects to conserve vital water supplies and we have money to build hospitals. For myself, I've learned a lot too and my involvement in Fairtrade has taken me to many places. For example, I never imagined I would get a chance to visit the UK and South Africa. I now know what it takes to produce good tea and coffee, so I am working to sell good quality products not just from Kenya but from across East Africa. I want farmers to get paid so that they don't think that their toiling is a cycle of poverty, and I will try everything possible to get them better prices and to connect them as much as I can. One of my buyers is from Russia. He wanted coffee from Uganda and I was able to say, no problem, I know people - and I do. Now I know tea and coffee farmers all over Africa because of the Fairtrade convention, and if by my intervention I can get those farmers a better price and their workers a better quality of life, then I'll be happy.

19   *Loved despite our differences*

Soroush Sadeghzadeh

Soroush Sadeghzadeh came to the UK 12 years ago as an asylum-seeker fleeing religious persecution in his native country, Iran. He now lives in Teesside where he manages the Middlesbrough Foodbank, based at the St Cuthbert's Centre on Whitehouse Street, West Lane.

'For I was hungry and you gave me food, I was thirsty and you gave me something to drink, I was a stranger and you welcomed me, I was naked and you gave me clothing' (Matthew 25:35).

John Sentamu writes:

In Christ's teaching on God's final judgement of the nations when people will be separated like a shepherd separates the sheep from the goats, he tells his listeners that our love or indifference to him will be measured by the way we treat those in need – for each one of them is a stand-in-for-Jesus Christ himself.

As we care for the needs of the least of his brothers and sisters, we are showing that same love and care for Jesus Christ. If we ignore them, and turn from them, we do the same to Him. We must *'love the Lord with all our heart, with all our soul, with all our mind and with all our strength'* and *'love our neighbours as ourselves'* (Mark 12:30-31).

Soroush has experienced this kind of love both as a receiver and as a giver. When his life was dislocated by the persecution of his Christian faith in Iran, he had to leave all that he knew there, and seek asylum in the UK. There were times of difficulty and strangeness, but his love for God drew him to look out for ways to become involved in his new community.

Encouraged by the love and welcome of people in his church in Middlesbrough, he was able to bring God's love and care for others who had been driven to seek asylum and refuge. God's love for us is ever renewed as we pour it out and share it.

✠

I'd been married for less than three weeks when my father took me aside and said that it was no longer safe for me to stay in Iran. At 18 years old I had already suffered years of persecution because of my Christian faith. As a teenager I was arrested many times, harshly interrogated and tortured. Each time I was arrested my father spoke to officials on my behalf and bailed me out, but the day he came to tell me to leave we'd separately received warnings that next time would be different. We both knew these threats were serious and what the consequences would be if I stayed. When we spoke my father had already made travel arrangements for my wife Mahvash and me to leave the country, and the next day we boarded a plane, knowing we might never return.

While waiting for our case for asylum to be heard we were dispersed to Middlesbrough, where we were given a flat and a weekly allowance to live on. Next door lived another family who had also come to the UK seeking asylum. We were safe, but at the same time life felt very strange. In Iran we'd grown used to being followed and having every telephone conversation monitored. Here nobody was following us and we didn't need to worry about how we might make a private telephone call. We could walk into a church and pray whenever we wanted. Sometimes I'd look around at other people in the church and wonder if they realised just what wonderful freedoms they had; if they were aware of the risks people take in some other parts of the world to be able to come together to pray and worship God.

For the first few months, while we were waiting for our case to be heard, there wasn't much we could do other than adjust to living in a different culture and, more than anything, get accustomed to the weather. Although grateful to be safe, we felt somewhat useless and hoped that we might find a church where we could settle and contribute. One day Mahvash mentioned this to a man she met while in Middlesbrough town centre. Although she didn't know it before they spoke, the man was one of the leaders of Jubilee Church Teesside. He invited us to go along and on the following Sunday someone from the church picked us up at our house and drove us to the service. I remember thinking how comfortable it was. In Iran sometimes we would walk miles into the mountains to worship, because in the winter we knew that no one would want to follow us there – it was too cold.

It was great to not have to hide what we were doing any more but the style of worship was so different to what I'd been used to that it took me by surprise. Here people were playing drums and electric guitars as part of the service. Having grown up in a culture that didn't allow musical instruments the service was a bit challenging to me at first, but as I was praying God put it in my heart to not be frightened by the differences and to instead focus on how we were accepted into the church even though we were different. That acceptance was a wonderful thing and the welcome we received made us feel as though we were already part of the church. For the first time since arriving in the UK I felt like we belonged, as if we had found a family who cared for us.

Being away from our families and not having that support was difficult. It was clear that we were very different to most of the people around us. We looked different and we spoke differently. I remember being on a bus on the way to Middlesbrough town centre when my phone rang – it was my family calling from Iran. I answered and naturally started speaking in my native tongue, but almost as soon as I spoke I became aware of people turning to look at me. For some people our difference must have seemed threatening because we hadn't been in our new home long when someone threw a brick through the window. Sadly, this incident wasn't a one-off. Once we had been granted asylum and were allowed to work we bought a car, but almost as soon as we brought it home it was smashed. This vandalism didn't happen to everyone in the street, so we wanted to find out the reasons behind it. Why us? Was it that particular people didn't like us, because if it was we didn't know who it could be or who we could have offended? We had made good friends with many people in the area where we lived and most of our neighbours were very friendly towards us. When we asked why this was happening our friends said it might be because we are different. They helped us to get the police involved, who explained that it was nothing personal or anything we'd done. These were crimes of racial hatred and we'd been targeted for no other reason than we were different.

These incidents made us think that perhaps Middlesbrough wasn't the right place for us to live and that we needed to move somewhere more ethnically diverse, like London, where we thought we wouldn't stand out as being so different. We started searching on the internet for somewhere else to live but everything in the country was new to us and we didn't know where to start, where to go or what to do.

Through Jubilee Church we were introduced to the charity Open Door North East, a Christian charity serving asylum seekers and refugees in the Tees Valley region. When we told them what was happening they tried to give us some support in how to deal with it, but as the harassment escalated it was clear that we needed to move away from the situation, so they helped us to find another house in a different part of Teesside.

Although we wanted to move house it was heart-breaking to think that we were moving away from the good friends we had made in the area, and the emotional as well as the practical support we got from Open Door meant a lot to us at that time. The staff listened to us, they sympathised and explained the whole process of how to find a house to rent in the UK – where to go, what to do, how much it might cost, what things to take into account when you move house and all sorts of things that we would never have thought of. The charity was helpful in giving us the bigger picture on how house-hunting works here and through that we were able to get in touch with an agency who found us a house. Once we did that everything felt far more straightforward; we went to view the house, it was right for us, and we moved in.

Now we'd been granted asylum we were refugees and could move anywhere we wanted to in the country. You might think that we would have chosen to move out of Teesside but we decided to stay. Anyone can experience abuse in any part of the world, because there will always be people who express themselves and their opinions in aggressive ways. I strongly believe that God didn't bring us here simply to be out of the danger zone and have a safe life. He brought us here for a reason and I believe that he wants us to contribute to society and play our part in the community in which we find ourselves.

The help Open Door North East gave to us was important in helping us to feel settled and because of that we wanted to support and be part of its work in any way we could. Sometime later I was offered a part-time job at Open Door to help set up a Night Shelter for destitute asylum seekers. I think they thought that a refugee would probably have a better insight into what it is like for a person to go through this process. Thankfully I've never experienced destitution in the UK, but

I had been through the process of claiming asylum and I knew that it was intense and can be difficult at times.

After that I took on another project with the charity called Work Club, which helped refugees find work suited to their skills, enabling them to contribute to society in the best way they can. I made lots of friends doing that job and every day was exciting. Mahvesh now does a similar job, helping refugees get their skills up to speed so that they are in a better position to find employment, and we both volunteer doing things like translating documents and helping with fundraising.

I worked at Open Door for a number of years and the charity is still very close to our hearts. Mahvesh works there now and I volunteer, to stay involved. However, I felt that while I loved my work there, God was calling me to be more involved with the local people and not just a specific group of people. When I heard about the job at the Food Bank I felt moved to apply and I was blessed to be offered it. I'm so glad I was because the role is a real blessing for me and God has given me a vision for it to take the work forward.

My work at Middlesbrough Food Bank is similar to the work I did at Open Door in that it's the kind of job where you need to be fully committed with your heart to be able to give it the best you can. It is a big operation. Each week we put together about 100 emergency food parcels, which are then distributed across the town via churches and other organisations that rely on the charity to offer support to people in crisis. I'm always amazed at the generosity of people who donate so much food to us, week in and week out. At the same time, it is heart-breaking to know that this huge amount of food won't last us very long. The food flies off the shelves because the need is so great and unfortunately that need is growing. I've had calls from people who've told me that they haven't eaten for two days. It's heart-breaking, but the fact that God has provided for us to be able to do this work is a great thing because, while we hope people won't always be in this difficult financial situation, at least for now we can respond and say there is some help available.

When I look back, I can see that God had a great plan for us in this area. I am now 32 years old and have lived in the UK for 12 years. It was very difficult for us at the beginning because everything was new and we missed our families. Family means a lot to us, as I'm sure it does to people everywhere. During our time here God has opened our eyes to our God-given family, particularly the people in our church who have loved us so dearly that it feels like they are our family. It is as if God, hearing our cries, has given us a family even greater in number.

Since we have lived in the UK, Mahvesh's mother has visited us once and I saw my family recently for the first time in 12 years when they travelled to Turkey. Thankfully we are still in contact. Making a telephone call home isn't a problem but some phones in Iran are monitored so we have to be careful about what we say about our whereabouts and what we share.

I pray that one day I will be able to visit Iran because it is where I grew up and all my childhood memories are there. At the same time, it is difficult to call it home because Teesside is our home now and even the thought of moving away from here brings tears to my eyes. For us, Teesside is our home because God has made it home to us. If we'd had a choice at the beginning, we probably wouldn't have chosen to live here; now we wouldn't want to be anywhere else, and that is because of the church and people. They have welcomed and loved us despite our differences.

20   An open home

David Tomlinson

The Reverend David Tomlinson is vicar of St John's Parish church in Shildon, County Durham. Before ordination he and his wife Davina lived with an open house in the west of Scotland for nine years, helping people from all walks of life who found themselves in need. The couple, who have two grown-up children, continue to be strong advocates of expressing faith through works of love in the community, including running food aid projects, a credit union, a drug and alcohol drop-in centre, and community gardens in the parish where they now live. They are active foster carers and have fostered more than 60 children.

'Is not this the fast that I choose: to loose the bonds of injustice, to undo the thongs of the yoke, to let the oppressed go free, and to break every yoke? Is it not to share your bread with the hungry, and bring

the homeless poor into your house; when you see the
naked, to cover them, and not to hide yourself from
your own kin?' (Isaiah 58: 6-7).

John Sentamu writes:

In Isaiah, the Lord is calling his people to turn from empty displays of religion, and is challenging them to repent of their indifference to injustice and the needs of the poor. True worship and love of the Lord, he says, are demonstrated in lives of love and care for others. That is the fast the Lord would choose.

David's story shows how he and his family have tried to live out these words of Isaiah in the kind of sacrificial life to which God called them.

It is not a way of life which comes easily to us and it may be misunderstood by others – as David found when he was looking after people who seemed strange to his neighbours. But God is always with us, and David and his family have clearly discovered the truth of Hebrews 13:2, *'Do not neglect to show hospitality to strangers, for by doing that some have entertained angels without knowing it.'*

Praise God that David's 'angels' - the adults and children transformed by their love and care – have brought joy and blessing to the whole family, and have helped build greater acceptance and understanding in the community.

✣

There's a passage in the Bible where the Prophet Isaiah talks about true fasting for those eager to seek God, only it is not the kind of religious fasting the Israelites were used to. At the time it was common for religious people to abstain from food, bow their heads and lie in sackcloth and ashes as ways of getting closer to God. The same people who strictly followed those rituals often turned their eyes from the needs of those around them, particularly the hungry and oppressed, and then wondered why God felt distant from them. Isaiah showed a way to fast that was more pleasing to the Lord. It is not about depriving ourselves but rather sharing what we have with others who are less fortunate. In my life perhaps I have taken that passage more literally than most.

As an expression of our faith my wife Davina and I lived for years with an open home. In many ways I've always been an idealist and for us opening our home to people in need was a way of living out those scriptures and exploring what community means. The decision wasn't something that we arrived at overnight. For a long time we had invited people to eat with us on most days. Opening our home for people to stay felt like an extension of that hospitality. I felt very much that if I had something I wanted to share it with someone who didn't, and I was blessed that Davina and our two children were willing to share this view.

My career in retail management had bought us a good lifestyle, but I wasn't happy. As my thirties approached I wanted something different and began to have a sense of God calling us to a new way of being and living. After talking it over with Davina we put our house up for sale and moved to Torrisdale on the west coast of Scotland, where at that time we could buy a bigger house, renovate it and still have some money left from the sale of our house to tide us over while we got settled.

The intention of moving was always to live with an open home. We bought a three-bedroomed bungalow with a craft shop attached. The property was semi-derelict at the time, so, as we needed to do building work anyway, we took the opportunity to extend the bungalow and convert the loft to give us a six-bedroom family home. We were able to extend the garden too, managing to purchase three acres of rough ground surrounding the bungalow, which gave us a wonderful sense of space.

Our nearest neighbour was a farm about one and a half miles away and people who knew us would say, 'How do you manage being so isolated?' Life in Torrisdale was very different to what we'd been used to, but to us, our home never felt isolated because there was so much natural beauty all around us. Within three minutes' walk we'd be on the beach, where seals played and there were caves to explore. We kept chickens and ducks, which provided us with fresh eggs. We grew our own fruit and vegetables, baked our own bread and made trips to Campbeltown, twelve miles away, to stock up our cupboards and freezer with foodstuffs, quickly learning which milk we could and couldn't freeze.

Once settled, I began to write magazine articles about our vision for the house, and people started to come. At first we mainly welcomed people who had been sleeping rough, but it wasn't long before we found ourselves sharing our home with people in all kinds of need – women who were fleeing domestic abuse, families who had been flooded from their homes, ex-military personnel who had returned from war zones and were experiencing post-traumatic stress, people who had recently been released from prison, people who were recovering from a mental breakdown, and people with learning disabilities whose families needed someone to provide respite care. Some people stayed with us for a few days, others a few months. We survived financially through prayer, gifts, and people who stayed giving what they could.

Not everyone embraced our new way of life, and it was clear that many people in the community, even though we were members of the local church, held us in suspicion. They thought that we were bringing strange and dangerous people into the area, because people who are struggling often look a little bit odd. Thankfully there were also people who welcomed what we were doing, particularly organisations like the council whose job it was to help people in need. It wasn't long before the local social services started sending people our way, and from then as soon as a bed became free there was someone else to fill it. When the house was full we even had people staying in a caravan parked on our land.

The caravan was loaned to us by the Salvation Army, who on hearing what we were doing said that if we looked after the caravan we could use it whenever we wanted. So, the Salvation Army parked the caravan in our garden, and we often had young men living there.

We'd been living like this for several years when we got a call from the social work department asking if we could take in a young woman who was sleeping rough. It was only after we'd said, 'Yes, of course,' that we found out she was only fifteen years old.

You could say that we became foster carers by default, because for us, it wasn't so much that we said: 'Let's become foster carers', as we thought, there are some folk here who need support, encouragement and care – we can provide that.

It took us by surprise how many children, just within the Argyll and Bute area, were in desperate need of a loving home. We signed up as short-term foster carers, which could mean anything up to three years. Depending on the situation sometimes children stayed longer and we cared for a wonderful young girl, who is still very much a part of our lives today, for six years until she moved into a home of her own as an adult.

The children brought such life to the house, filling it with noise, laughter, chaos, tantrums and the whole vibrancy of life that goes with it. The liveliness often helped many of the adults who stayed with us, but over time it became clear that if we were going to foster more children then we couldn't support adults in the way we had done previously. There was a safeguarding issue with some of the people who stayed with us and we had a sad incident of someone severely self-harming, and although, thankfully, none of the children witnessed it, we felt that our focus needed to change.

Our own children were aged six and eight when we first started fostering. We tried hard to not foster children who were the age of our children. It didn't always work out that way, but in the main when our children were smaller we had a lot of teenagers in the house and when they were older we fostered a lot of younger children.

In places where there is a small population, often everybody knows everybody else and we knew most of the people who lived along the road between us and Campbeltown, and most people knew us. Many of the teenagers who were placed with us came from the local area and many people knew them as well, generally for being challenging to live with. When people saw these troubled teens living with us and getting along fine, often their view of what we were doing changed and we began to be greeted warmly all over the place. There were always people who were good to us, but we now felt a genuine sense of neighbourliness.

People were kind in such unexpected ways. Once we had our car stolen, which was a bizarre occurrence in an area with very little crime. It was a young man who took it. He had been at a party in Carradale and was walking 16 miles home to Campbeltown. Four miles into his journey he stumbled upon our house. The doors were always open so he walked in, took the car keys and drove off in our car. He didn't get very far, crashing it into a bridge just around the corner, but although we got it back, because it was an old car the damage was more than the car was worth.

For a remote place there was a lot going on socially and the children were always all involved in different activities, like the dramatic society, sea cadets and swimming club, which meant a lot of ferrying them around in the car. The local garage owner knew this and gave us the loan of a car for weeks and weeks, even though he knew that we wouldn't have the money to buy a new car from him when we handed it back.

There were other times when we were able to be the ones to help. We often had power cuts in the area, and one Christmas we were the only ones, within several miles, whose electricity was still on. People who lived in Carradale Village to the north of us and from Saddell, a little hamlet on the other side, brought flasks to us throughout the day so that we could fill them with hot water. That was the way folk lived – people helped each other and because of that there was a great sense of community, a feeling of being wanted, loved and cared for. There was a constant sharing of resources and abilities, which the children became a part of. The farmers were always welcoming towards the children, and the children were always keen to get involved in helping with the work on the land. In lambing season they would help deliver the lambs, and during ploughing season they helped out by picking stones from the fields. This was how I had imagined living out community would be and there was a sense of the whole vibrancy of life that gave me far more back than I ever imagined.

Our life has been an adventure in faith. Davina and I have sought to live what we believe, and part of our journey is sharing who we are with others. Our home is wholly Christian in so far as we start and end the day with prayer, but people staying with us are always free to join in or not join in. We share our faith in the way we live as much as anything else. I think if your faith is open-hearted and you are welcoming people because you are welcoming them, loving people because you are loving them and not because you want to fix them, hopefully that expression of faith allows people to touch something that is precious and so explore their own spirituality in a way that works for them.

21 Break the chain of hate

Gee Walker

Dr Gee Walker's 18-year-old son Anthony was murdered on 29 July 2005 in an unprovoked racial attack at a park in Huyton, Merseyside. Out of her grief the Anthony Walker Foundation was born, a charity working to promote racial harmony through education, sport and the arts. In 2012 Gee was awarded an honorary Doctor of Laws from Liverpool University for her work with the Foundation, an honour she dedicated to Anthony.

'Do not be overcome by evil, but overcome evil with good' (Romans 12:21).

John Sentamu writes:

After writing stories about people's life struggles and challenges for fourteen years, the journalist Marina Cantacuzino set up The Forgiveness Project in 2004. Originally called The

F Word', it was a compilation and exhibition of photos and stories from people who had been deeply hurt or traumatized through violence, oppression or injustice and told of their journey towards forgiveness. All the participants spoke of the great effort forgiveness had cost them, but most also spoke of the sense of freedom and healing that forgiveness brought – for themselves, as well as for the perpetrators.

Gee's story tells us movingly about her own path out of the numbness and confusion she felt after her son's racially-motivated murder, and her acceptance of the freedom and peace which forgiveness can bring.

The Apostle Paul writes to the Romans to encourage them to rise above the evil that they suffer from others, and tells them to overcome that evil with good. Gee Walker has lived out that message as she chose to **'break the chain of hate'**, and to demonstrate that loving your enemy is not an unrealistic ideal, but a hard-won and positive way of giving meaning to hurting lives. For Jesus said, **'Love your enemies and pray for those who persecute you, so that you may be children of your heavenly Father in heaven ... He makes the sun rise on the evil and on the good, and sends rain on the righteous and the unrighteous ... Be perfect, therefore, as your heavenly Father is perfect'** (Matthew 5:44-45, 48). That is: do good, be loving, forgiving and merciful. And forgiveness is wrought in us as a gift by the Holy Spirit. And our God **'constantly forgives and forgets our sins and our not doing good'** because of the death and resurrection of Jesus Christ (Hebrews 10:17).

✛

When Anthony was 8 years old I showed him a photograph of me taking a jump shot and scoring with a slam dunk. I'd been having fun with youngsters on the University basketball court and someone had captured the moment I was mid-air, driving the ball through the hoop. I'd surprised myself and everyone watching with such a slick move. I don't think it was what anyone expected from a special needs teacher. The photograph was used in the University prospectus and I proudly took a copy home to show my kids. Anthony's gaze went from the photo to me and back again. 'Mum,' he said, 'if you can do that, so can I!'

From then on Anthony's world was basketball. I remember his first real basketball, the type the professionals use. He saved up every penny he had to buy that ball and once he got it, he took it everywhere; even when sleeping he kept his ball close by, carefully placed at the foot of his bed. We set up a net on the house wall for him to practice and everywhere he went he'd be bouncing a ball. I worried that one day his ball might roll into the road and he'd run in front of a car, so I gave him a carrier bag to put his ball in on the way to the park. When that didn't work I even bought a designer sports bag for him to carry the ball in, but he never did. If ever I couldn't find him, I never had far to look. If he wasn't at home shooting hoops, Anthony was bouncing his ball in the park – after school, after church, on holidays he'd be there practising. 'It's going to be my career, Mum,' he said.

'Even if it is, these things are temporary,' I told him. 'You can't play basketball your whole life, you need something else to fall back on; you need your schooling.'

'Okay, Mum,' he said, 'I think I might like to be a lawyer because then I could help to make things fairer for people. Do you think I could be a lawyer and play basketball?'

I think his idea came partly from watching Will Smith in *The Fresh Prince of Bel-Air* and wanting to be like him, but it also arose from a strong sense of justice within him and true to his word Anthony followed both dreams, signing up for A level law at college while bouncing his ball everywhere he went.

Being the eldest son of six children in a single-parent household Anthony naturally took on a sense of responsibility that I never expected from him. When we needed an upgrade on the car he got a weekend job serving in McDonald's and handing me his first pay packet said: 'Let's get a car.'

'Don't you worry about my car,' I told him, but he wanted to help and while £50 wasn't enough to pay for a car it was enough for a deposit, so we went together to choose one. There were many other times too when he'd help me out without my asking. I'd put my hand into my pocket and think where did that money come from? It would be Anthony, always making sure I was all right even when I refused to take any money from him. He always gave a thought for other people before himself.

When I asked him to babysit that night, he didn't tell me that he'd been invited to his end of year college party, he just agreed. I felt bad about that for a long time, but we all have ifs and buts, things we tell ourselves that we could have or should have done.

Instead of joining the other students at the party, Anthony stayed in to babysit for his sister's two young children, helped by his friend Louise and cousin Marcus. At 11pm the three of them left the house to walk to the bus stop where Louise would catch her bus home. I was upstairs with the babies and didn't hear them shout to say they were leaving. When I got downstairs they had already gone and I looked out of the window to see them walking down the road. I thought that they were only walking to the bus stop at the end of the street and wouldn't be long.

Soon after they left the phone rang. It was Marcus, but I couldn't understand what he was saying. Something about Anthony being attacked; it didn't make any sense. A female voice came on the line. 'Just get to Whiston Hospital,' she said. I arranged for my other two children to look after my grandchildren and went straight to the accident and emergency department. The hospital was busy. I arrived before Anthony and no one could tell me what had happened. Lots of ambulances were arriving and leaving. Each time I'd look to see if it was Anthony they were bringing in and when it wasn't I'd be looking with the same anticipation when the next one arrived.

The hospital staff kept asking if I was on my own and if I could get someone to be with me. While I was waiting a nurse came over to me and this time was more direct: 'You need someone with you,' she said.

'I don't have anyone. My children are babysitting or at work.'

'What about your husband?' she asked.

'We've been separated for years.'

'Isn't there anyone you can ask to come?'

'I'll be good, I'm okay,' I assured her. I didn't want to wake anyone at that time of night, but the nurse was insistent, so I called my aunt, who agreed to come, and the hospital sent a taxi to collect her.

While I was waiting another nurse sat and prayed with me and I began to feel a sense of peace. I was told that Anthony had arrived but I wasn't allowed to see him. There was only one bar of power left on my mobile phone and I used the last drop of it to call every pastor I knew. Once I'd done that I believed that everything was going to be all right because everyone was praying. Even when the doctor came to see me and said, 'It's bad, Mrs Walker.' I replied, 'How bad can it get? I want to see my son. I need to see my child.'

Drops of blood led me to where Anthony was and I'm glad my other children were protected from what I was about to see. The doctors had covered the weapon, but it was still in Anthony's head. It was a mountaineering axe, and the handle was between two to three feet long. I wasn't allowed to touch my son in the hospital, but I have to hope he knew I was there. Five hours after arriving in the ambulance Anthony was dead.

My daughters tell me that I didn't speak for a week after that, unless I had to. I wasn't aware of it at the time, but it was like I was at home with the lights out. I think that quiet time was my time with God, just me and him.

During the investigation my daughter, Dominique who was 20 years old at the time told a reporter, 'Seventy times seven we have to forgive', that's what Jesus said. So we have to, we have to forgive. For me, I know, it's hard. Every day, every day, it's an everyday thing. That's what my mum says, it's an everyday thing.' My initial thoughts were that Dominique shouldn't have gone out and told everybody. It felt like she was telling our family secrets, things that should just be between us. Later that day when we were back at home I walked over to Dominique and gave her a hug. It was as if hearing her say those words from the Bible was the catalyst that sparked a change in me because as we held each other I started talking again.

People often say to me, 'Where was God in all this?' and I say, 'He was right there holding me up, like he promised'. God didn't kill my son, hate did and that's got no place in my heart, or my family or my life. I saw what hate can do and I don't want any part of it.

We buried Anthony on 25 August 2005 and I laid his basketball alongside him in his coffin. More than 3,000 mourners came to Liverpool Cathedral for his funeral and the service was also broadcast live on a city centre screen. By this time Paul Taylor, aged 20, and his cousin, Michael Barton, aged 17, had been arrested and charged with Anthony's murder. I thought what happened couldn't be more shocking and then I learned that the people who did it were known to my family. They went to the same school as my children and would have played together in primary school. The men who killed Anthony said that they didn't know it was him. What difference does that make? They killed a man and they intended to do it. If it hadn't been Anthony it would have been someone else's child.

When Anthony, Marcus and Louise got to the bus stop that night they were subjected to a tirade of racist abuse. Not one for confrontations, Anthony chose to walk away and took a short-cut through the park he loved to get to the next bus stop. The two who had been hurling abuse continued to pursue them in a car, driving to the park entrance where they hid in bushes, ready to ambush Anthony and his friends as they walked past. Without warning the two men jumped out in front of them brandishing an axe. Louise and Marcus ran managing to escape, but Anthony was trapped and I saw what they did to him with that axe.

Standing outside the court, after hearing the guilty verdicts, I said: 'My family and I still stand by what we believe: forgiveness.' I can still see the expression on the journalist's face. It was like she thought I'd lost the plot. I asked my daughter, Dominique: 'What did I just say to her?'

'You said you forgive.'

Did I really say that? All I can think is it's one of those moments where what's in the heart comes out of the mouth. People said to me, was it hard to forgive? For me, no, it wasn't, because it was how I lived my whole life. Say I chose to hate and seek revenge, what would that do? It would seemingly bring a temporary victory but I'd live and I wouldn't have any peace in myself because that would make me just like them, creating a chain of hate, reinforcing the pain and hurt they have caused. When you lose a child you're in turmoil. It's hard, like you're on fire all the time; you hurt and there's no medication for it. You see someone on the street and want to shout out to your kid but it's not your kid; you go shopping and pick up stuff that they would like – ten years on and I still do that for Anthony.

I see forgiveness as a gift. It's a gift to me wrapped up in peace and it's something that can't be bought. It's not about Anthony's killers; it's about freeing myself up to process my pain and what I'm going through, because carrying their hate would destroy me, my sleep and my health – as if I haven't got enough to contend with. I can't take any more, so let them keep their hate and I'll bask in the peace forgiveness gives me.

Some people hate without reason and some of that hatred is learned behaviour. Some people hate because it gives them something to do or because of something that happened in the past, and other people hate because of peer pressure and they follow a crowd. It's a blind revenge and it's misleading; thinking revenge is the answer when it isn't. They see what's in front of them, not the bigger picture. Forgiveness is a choice. People blame God for a lot of bad things when it's down to us, human beings, to do what's right. God has given us free will and we can all choose to do what is right. Someone must be conscious enough to break the chain of hate. As Anthony would say, somebody has got to show them, Mum. Unfortunately that someone is me.

Not long after the trial people started asking me what I was going to do about Anthony. I'd say, 'What are you talking about? What am I supposed to do? Isn't it enough that they've taken my child? What more do you want from me?' There was talk about charities and foundations and I'd say, 'Look I don't know anything about anything.' Then money started coming in and I didn't know what to do. I didn't realise that people were donating money to help us as a family, so we used that money to start the Anthony Walker Foundation in 2006.

I couldn't carry on with my teaching job so I'd started doing learning support instead. Through my connection with schools I began speaking in RE classes about forgiveness. One school called another, spreading the word about what I was doing, so that before long I had lots of requests to speak. Over the years the Foundation has grown. Now it's a team of people with passion who come together to promote racial harmony. As well as talks and workshops we support the Anthony Walker Law Bursary with the Crown Prosecution Service and Liverpool John Moores University, aimed at supporting young people from disadvantaged backgrounds to work in law, like Anthony wanted to do. We also organise an annual festival and a basketball competition. When people talk about bringing community together, the festival does just that. Normally I find a space where I can sit back and watch – I can't express the joy it gives me to see the delight on the young people's faces. When I see young people enjoying something Anthony would have done, I see a piece of him in each one of them.

In 2012 I gratefully received an honorary Doctor of Laws from Liverpool University for my work promoting racial equality through the Foundation. I dedicated that degree to Anthony. When your heart has been broken into a million pieces, how can you come back from that? By God's grace I am able to, but I cannot move on because I ache every day. I want my boy back but I know I'll never get him back. By God's grace I carry on, and I'm learning to process my pain by doing what Anthony would have wanted to do. My son was born to be a great man and I can't allow that greatness to die.

People ask me, when am I going to stop, don't I get tired? I say, 'I'll stop when I know no one is listening'. Not long ago I spoke at a conference with three other mothers who had lost children. I talked about my view of forgiveness and what it's done for me. People have the misunderstanding that forgiveness is forgetting, not caring, letting someone off the hook, and it's not. How can I forget my pain? I can't and that's not my choice; but at the same time I can't share my space with hate and that is my choice. My reward is a peace that I can't explain, but I know is there. It has enabled me to carry on and function so that I don't drive people away. When people are full of hate I don't think they realise they are projecting that hatred, people can feel it and it drives them away. I don't want that to happen to me. When my grandchildren come into the room I want them to see love and feel love. People learn by example. How am I supposed to encourage my kids to be good people if I talk one way and live another? I'm not saying I forgive because I have to but because I live it and surely if I'm showing you through my life, you can see it's not impossible, it can be done.

As I was talking at the conference, one of the other mothers who had said she felt full of hate began moving closer to me. She got closer and closer until her head was resting on my shoulder and then she began to cry. It was like something broke inside of her and she said to me, 'You know what, Gee, I'm going to go home and try this forgiveness thing'. I heard that mother has since died, but when I'm feeling tired and tempted to stop, I think about her. I don't know what happened, but something changed in her that day. Experiences like that help me to carry on, because what I do and what we do as a Foundation is Anthony's legacy and it's changing lives.

22   *Another door*

Irene Wilson

The Reverend Irene Wilson was involved in a head-on car crash in 2004 which left her badly injured and unable to return to her job as a special needs teacher. At a time when it looked like everything she'd known was being taken from her, a new opportunity opened. Irene was ordained in 2011 and now heads up pastoral care at Holy Trinity Church in Hull where she has established a weekly soup run in the city centre.

'For surely I know the plans I have for you', says the Lord, 'plans for your welfare and not for harm, to give you a future with hope' (Jeremiah 29:11).

John Sentamu writes:

Do you like to make plans – maybe for your holidays, DIY projects, promotion at work? Most of us like to make plans as they give us a feeling of control and purpose in our lives, a sense that we know where we're going.

When our plans are derailed we can be left confused and uncertain about who we are and what our life is about. But, as the Bible reminds us, *'The mind of man plans his way, But the Lord directs his steps'* (Proverbs 16:9). I have learnt the hard way that if you want to make God smile, tell him your plans!

Irene's life plan was thrown off track by her car accident, but God showed her that he still had good things in mind for her life. How wonderful to know that God can open new doors for us, if only we are willing to go through. Door after door opened for Irene, showing her the way God wanted her to travel.

Though the accident seemed like a tragedy at the time, God's ultimate plans were for good and not for harm. They have brought Irene a life which blesses others, and given her a future with hope. If we will listen to Him, God's love always directs us into ways of blessing. And Jesus promised *'to be with us till the end of the age'* (Matthew 28:2b). Therefore, *'Rejoice always, pray without ceasing, giving thanks in all circumstances; for this is the will of God in Christ Jesus for you'* (1 Thessalonians 5:16-17).

☩

I never imagined that I'd give up teaching, not before retirement anyway. For many years I worked in a school for children with severe learning difficulties. I've always been drawn to people who need a little bit of extra care and for me it was a great job that I enjoyed. At the end of term I said goodbye and thought I'd be back with everyone, the same as always, to start the new term. During the break I was going to France with my husband, Ian. While on holiday we were involved in a head-on car crash, and I never returned to work after that.

Fortunately I didn't have internal injuries, but my legs were smashed and my jaw was very badly broken. Physically, Ian escaped the crash with only bruising, but he was very emotionally damaged by it and his life changed dramatically too. Suddenly I needed a lot of care. It took almost two years of rehabilitation for me to be able to begin walking again, which I can now do with the aid of a stick.

Once I was able to get around independently I started busying myself with work in the parish where I was training to be a Reader. As I improved physically, a vacancy arose within the parish and I felt drawn to consider ordination. I wanted to pursue it but didn't feel confident enough to suggest it because I couldn't imagine ever being accepted. One day I mentioned it to the vicar of a nearby village who was a friend of mine. 'Do you think I would ever be able to become a deacon?' I asked, cautiously.

'Of course,' she said and I could tell by the enthusiasm and encouragement in her voice that, for her, perhaps this wasn't such a ridiculous idea. From then on doors kept opening for me. I couldn't believe that I was being given such an opportunity at this late stage of my life – it was amazing. We live in a small village in the west of Hull and I thought perhaps after ordination I might be offered some work in the village or in school ministry. When a placement came up in the city centre of Hull it felt like the icing was being put on my cake. I was 60 years old and here was an opportunity for me to do something completely new.

Not long after I'd started in ministry a young girl at church told me about a man she'd seen sleeping in a doorway. It is a sight that sadly many of us have grown used to and feel helpless to do anything about, but this girl was deeply moved to the point of being compelled to take action, anything to try to help. 'I want to take him some soup,' she said with both the naivety and courage of the young. Being new to city-centre life, I too was naive in so far as I hadn't considered that there were so many people sleeping rough. It was winter and I shared this girl's view that perhaps if we could bring some comfort, however small, to one person, at least we would have done something. I glanced at Ian and he took the initiative to respond. 'If you're going, then we're coming too,' he said.

That first night we felt like real novices. There were four of us: myself, Ian, the young girl and her mother. We set off at about 11pm, walking the streets of Hull city centre, carrying paper cups and flasks filled with hot soup. The young girl directed us to the doorway where she'd seen the man sleeping and there he was, only a young laddie himself. 'Would you like some soup?' I asked. He looked surprised but accepted gladly. We chatted for a while, but he didn't give away much information about himself. We did learn, however, that in order to find a dry, sheltered space to sleep, he usually settled down much earlier in the evening. We said that we'd come back to see him again, and said we wouldn't be as late next time

On our way back to the car we took a winding route through the city's streets. Wherever we came across people sleeping rough we offered them soup, just as we had done with that first young man, but it soon became clear that the flasks we were carrying couldn't hold enough soup to give some to everyone we saw. I hadn't been aware of just how much of a problem homelessness was. My reaction was to do what I could at that moment in time for that one person in front of me. Many people said to me: 'Aren't you just making it worse? If you stopped feeding them they would go and find something else to do,' or 'If you stopped feeding them they'd have to sort themselves out.' I was conscious of not wanting to encourage rough sleeping, because it is not the type of situation you would want anyone to be in. At the same time I thought about the people we'd been meeting, they were happy to see us and wanted to see us. Sometimes I wished that people would take a step back and think beyond what they see, especially when what they see isn't very good. Difficult circumstances are much easier to get into than get out of. If a person has no love and support, what are they to do?

It is only as I've got older that I've begun to appreciate the love, care and support I got from my family. My family never had much money but there was always a lot of love to go around. My dad worked hard as a labourer all week. On Sunday lunchtime he would go to the pub and on his way home he'd call into the local sweetshop to buy a box of chocolates for my mother and a bag of sweets each for me and my sister. Walking down the lane towards our house he would always empty his pockets of change, throwing any coins he had to the kids playing in the street. For us it was the same pattern every weekend, but my father's childhood hadn't been so fortunate. His father was drowned at sea. His mother remarried, but his stepfather was an abusive man and my father left home to live with his sister. A few years later his mother died of cancer and as soon as he was old enough my father left his sister's house to join the navy. When I think about it now, my father had a bit of a drinking problem, although we didn't see it that way at the time, because people weren't as open to talk about things like that in those days. Looking back, it wouldn't be surprising if he did, because my father had such a troubled life in many ways. At the same time he was such a generous and loving person. I wonder how different his life might have been without my mother there to support him and without the love of our family. All that love – I think we often don't appreciate it until much further down the road.

I decided to find out about the other agencies working with homeless people in the city and the work they were doing, how we could work with them, and the kind of things that would be most useful for us to do. Using that information we decided to set up our soup stall in a central place and on a regular basis, so that it would be easy for people to find us. What we do is still very basic. We go to a car park on Tuesday and Thursday each week and give out soup, sandwiches, tea and coffee to between 20 and 30 people. We don't have any special equipment – we stand the catering flasks in our car boot and use a torch for a lamp.

On hearing about what we were doing other people began to step in to help in many different ways such as joining us on a soup run, providing food or offering prayer. The Roman

Catholic church offered to do the same on a different night of the week because we wanted to make sure that there was always something available every day and we weren't duplicating our effort. Some of the outreach workers from the local hostel, Dock House, came to join us and we work closely with them now, because they can help us to direct people to safe places where they can get medical advice or shelter.

We don't always know what happens to the people we meet. They stop coming and we hope that they've moved on. That first young laddie got a flat after about 18 months and thankfully hasn't returned to the streets. There are other people who we help so far and then we go out one night and see them on the streets again. It breaks my heart but I've got to accept that sometimes these things happen. We mustn't judge people for it, just help them start again.

One young chap, who had been coming to us from our early days, was offered a flat and he took it. Ian took him shopping to buy some basics to help furnish it. Once settled he came back to our soup run delighted to tell us that he'd got a job on the ferries. Then reaching in his pocket, he pulled out his wallet and handed me a £5 note. 'This is for you,' he said, 'You've helped me for so long, now I want to help the others.' It was great to see him and his gesture made us feel fantastic. We haven't seen him since, so we hope that he's still making a go of it.

In ministry, particularly city centre ministry, you can spend time with someone who will share everything that's going on in his life but never get to learn how it turned out, if any problems were resolved. It's the same with the people we meet on the streets and we just have to accept that we don't know. If we do bump into one of them in town and find they have moved on that's fantastic, but it doesn't always happen. There are a lot of people who we've met along the way but we don't know where they are now; we just hope that things have improved for them. The most important thing I've learned from my own life is not to be discouraged when things go wrong. No matter how old you are or what circumstances you find yourself in, there is always light. God is always there to open another door.